SCHOOL DEVELOPMENT SERIES
General Editors: David Hopkins and David Reynolds

AN INTRODUCTION TO TEACHER APPRAISAL

RYSJ

AN INTRODUCTION TO TEACHER APPRAISAL
A professional development approach

Rob Bollington
David Hopkins
Mel West

with a Foreword by
Howard Bradley

CASSELL

Cassell Educational Limited
Villiers House
41/47 Strand
London WC2N 5JE

First published 1990

British Library Cataloguing in Publication Data
Bollington, Rob
  An introduction to teacher appraisal: a professional
  development approach. – (School development series).
  1. Teachers. Assessment
  I. Title   II. Hopkins, David, *1949–*   III. West, Mel   IV.
  Series
  371.144

  ISBN 0–304–32252–0
  ISBN 0–304–31982–1 pbk

Typeset by Fakenham Photosetting Limited,
Fakenham, Norfolk

Printed and bound in Great Britain by Dotesios Printers Ltd, Trowbridge

CONTENTS

Foreword

We have only to listen to our own children when they return home from school to realize that no matter how perceptive and far-sighted the National Curriculum, no matter how well the school manipulates its funds under local management, the single most significant factor in a child's learning is the teacher. Children are quick to recognize and appreciate teachers whose enthusiasm shines through their work and whose skills can be observed in every interaction they have with a pupil. It is fortunate that so many teachers bring this professionalism to bear on their work because teachers are also the school's most expensive resource. In industry, any expensive piece of plant which had to perform a delicate task for 40 years and which had the capacity to make or mar the product would be the subject of constant care and attention. We have been very slow to realize in education circles that teachers need and deserve support, reassurance and encouragement to go on extending their skills and exploring the frontiers of their knowledge. That is why the introduction of appraisal is likely to have more far-reaching consequences for the success teachers have in their work than any other of the current crop of innovations.

Although a number of teachers had experimented with regular review meetings and others had been observed in the classroom by their colleagues as part of some scheme of shared teaching or curriculum development, the idea of a systematic scheme of appraisal covering all headteachers and teachers was slow to develop and when it did it emerged from an unlikely source – an industrial dispute. The publication of the ACAS working group report on appraisal was the first major turning point, leading as it did to the School Teacher Appraisal Pilot Study involving teachers in six LEAs. This pilot study allowed us for the first time to see schemes in action, to observe data gathering, to talk to those who had experience of appraisal interviews and to investigate the impact of the process on teachers in schools. Hoary myths were dispelled; now there were concrete issues to be handled. No longer had we to rely on the transposition of findings from industry which had doubtful transferability to schools: now we had our own direct experience. There emerged a style of appraisal which is unique in its professional orientation.

A great deal was learned by teachers in schools during the pilot study and my colleagues who wrote this book shared that knowledge as members of the evaluation team which was based at the Cambridge Institute. It was a great privilege for us to monitor the experience of hundreds of teachers and headteachers, as appraisees and appraisers. This book shares with readers coming new to the process some of that experience together with our reflections on it. I hope the book will help many schools and teachers to avoid some of the pitfalls, to select what is best from earlier models and, above all, to prepare themselves to make appraisal a satisfying and rewarding experience.

Howard Bradley,
Director of the Cambridge Institute of Education and of the Evaluation Team

Preface and Acknowledgements

Appraisal is increasingly becoming a feature of teachers' professional life. The purpose of this book is to assist all those involved in appraisal to develop and run the process. We provide advice based on a review of the appraisal literature, on our findings as members of the team evaluating the School Teacher Appraisal Pilot Study (STAPS) of 1987–9, and our work with teachers in developing schemes for appraisal. Each chapter of the book is devoted to an aspect of the appraisal process and contains a survey of experience from the literature and the pilot study, from which we derive key principles of guidance and advice.

We believe that a properly constructed and presented appraisal system can improve both the professional development of teachers and headteachers and the management of schools. We regard appraisal as one of a number of current initiatives, such as school development plans, the National Curriculum and records of achievement which, taken together, can significantly improve the quality of education in our schools. In our view appraisal can help teachers and headteachers order their priorities, improve their planning and contribute to professional development and school improvement. We believe that the developmental process of appraisal described in this book will support the work of teachers and headteachers at a time of change and development in the education system.

It was the experience gained from our involvement with the School Teacher Appraisal Pilot Study project that enabled us to write this book. We are therefore indebted to our friends and colleagues on that project for giving us that experience, challenging our assumptions and sharing their ideas and practice with us. The School Teacher Appraisal Pilot Study project was a unique experience of professional collaboration and we wish to acknowledge with gratitude the members of the National Steering Group, the National Development Centre and the co-ordinators, heads and teachers in the pilot LEAs. We are particularly grateful to our colleagues on the evaluation team Howard Bradley, Pam Carroll, Marion Dadds, Julie Howard and Geoff Southworth for supporting us in the production of this book and for collaboration on the project. Just when our families, Cindy and Lucy; Marloes and Jeroen; Clodagh, Jessie, Scarlett and Cameron realized that the project, and all the travelling it entailed, was finally over and that perhaps they might see a little more of us at mealtimes and weekends, we began work on this book. Without their forbearance we would not have been able to have done this or many other things. We hope that as we put down our pens for the last time and return home, to thank them in person, that they are still there.

Although we received much help and advice during the project and in the preparation of this book the perspective it adopts is our own. It goes without saying that the views expressed here do not commit our colleagues on the evaluation team, the National Steering Group or the Department of Education and Science. The views, like the errors of fact and interpretation, remain our own.

Rob Bollington, David Hopkins, Mel West, *Cambridge, October 1989*

Chapter 1

An Introduction to Teacher Appraisal

During the School Teacher Appraisal Pilot Study we asked a number of teachers why they thought appraisal was being introduced. Among the reasons given were to:

> improve teacher performance, increase job satisfaction, improve the delivery of INSET, and, ultimately and vitally, improve pupil performance;
>
> improve the standard of teaching and improve the quality of teaching;
>
> motivate teachers by indicating they are considered as individuals, highlight problems and difficulties and help solve them;
>
> increase professional awareness, to improve standards of teaching skills, curriculum, pupil and teacher performance, to formulate structured development of school, curriculum, teacher and pupils, to achieve value for money related to resources, buildings, staffing and in-service training, to identify needs.

> (Bradley *et al.*, 1988, pp. 6–8)

In these ways teachers indicated a range of purposes of appraisal, which went beyond the anticipated requirements. The teachers in question were among those surveyed during the evaluation of the School Teacher Appraisal Pilot Study. What they and others drew attention to was the variety of expectations about appraisal.

This chapter is intended to provide an analysis of these expectations. We do so through a survey of the historical background to appraisal in England and Wales and by considering the potential purposes of appraisal. We explore key principles which apply to the process and discuss the nature of the appraisal process. In doing this we also introduce the major theme of the book, which is our belief that appraisal should above all be conducted in the interests of enhancing the professional development of teachers.

THE BACKGROUND TO APPRAISAL

Over recent years appraisal schemes for teachers have increased in number. Some have been home-produced schemes, originated by individual heads, influenced by management and staff development training. Others have been part of official pilot studies, organized by LEAs. Notable among these have been the schemes operated as part of the School Teacher Appraisal Pilot Study. The picture remains a patchy and uneven one but there has been growing support for the introduction of developmental appraisal schemes. This momentum towards the introduction of developmental schemes of appraisal reflects a range of hopes and expectations about appraisal which are broadly positive. The feelings expressed by the teachers referred to earlier are indicative of this trend.

We now identify and discuss the various factors that have led to the introduction of

° Standards
° prof dev
° management

appraisal in the UK. First, appraisal can be regarded as a response to the desire to bring a greater degree of accountability into public services. Second, it can be seen as the culmination of a series of moves designed to improve the professional development of teachers and to identify more precisely their in-service training needs. Third, appraisal is also linked to attempts to develop the management of schools. At times there has been tension between these various pressures but our argument is that a properly constructed and managed professional appraisal scheme can enhance the development of teachers and, at the same time, provide reassurance to the general public that measures are in hand to improve the quality of education.

To return to our first factor, the introduction of appraisal can be said to reflect a climate in education, characterized by concern for improved quality, a greater degree of accountability and more efficiency, particularly in terms of use of resources. Within this climate has come the call for 'systematic performance appraisal, designed to bring about a better relationship between pay, responsibilities and performance, especially teaching performance in the class-room' (DES, 1985, pp. 55–6). Better management of the teaching force and more efficient identification of in-service training needs have been seen as potential outcomes of appraisal. The argument has been made that

> the regular and formal appraisal of the performance of all teachers is necessary if LEAs are to have the reliable, comprehensive and up-to-date information necessary for the systematic and effective provision of professional support and development and the deployment of staff to best advantage.
>
> (DES, 1985, p. 55)

In other words, appraisal has sometimes been put across, notably by central government, as a means of creating a more efficiently managed teaching force.

Second, teacher appraisal can be seen as arising from moves to develop teachers as professionals. The growth of in-service training for teachers, following the James Report (James, 1972) has coincided with a period of change and development in education. In this context, appraisal can be seen both as a form of in-service training and as a means of identifying further in-service training needs. In these respects it follows developments which have taken place as a result of other recent initiatives. In particular, TRIST (TVEI-Related In-service Training, TVEI being the Technical Vocational Education Initiative), GRIST (Grant-Related In-service Training) and LEATGS (LEA Training Grants Scheme) have taken teachers and LEAs part of the way along the road of identifying INSET needs more precisely. Appraisal can be seen as continuing this journey and adding greater sophistication to the process. It can also be seen as a method of providing support for those engaged in change and as a means of monitoring the effectiveness of INSET. Those arguing for appraisal on these grounds have come from across the broad spectrum of government and the educational world in general.

The same can be said about the third set of factors which has led to the introduction of appraisal: factors linked with the development of management techniques in education. Interest in appraisal has arisen as a result of the increased management training for senior staff and as a reflection of the requirements for schools and individuals to set out clearly their aims and objectives. From both these sources came an appreciation of the role of target setting and the growth of review interviews as occasions for monitoring and setting targets. Similarly, following the growth of whole-school review, individual review appeared the next logical step. The schemes registered by Turner and Clift (1985) can be seen largely as a result of these influences. Interestingly, schemes arising from these influences typically centre on interviews and tend not to depend on classroom observation. Such schemes tend to rely heavily on direct discussion between the head, perhaps supported by other colleagues in the school's senior management team, and individual teachers.

The various influences so far identified combined to create a 'case' for teacher appraisal. The movement towards appraisal was given momentum when the DES funded a study carried out by Suffolk LEA and published as *Those Having Torches* (Suffolk Education Department, 1985) and *In the Light of Torches* (Suffolk Education Department, 1987). This study drew developments together. Through a survey of current appraisal experience in the UK and overseas, particularly in North America, the Suffolk team was able to make a series of key recommendations on the principles and processes appraisal should ideally encompass. These recommendations influenced the Appraisal/Training Working Group set up by ACAS during the 1985 salary negotiations. This group, comprising representatives of teachers' associations, LEAs and the DES considered the principles and practicalities of a general appraisal scheme. In its report the group presented agreed principles which it felt should underpin such a scheme. It also considered the steps needed to prepare for the introduction of appraisal and recommended that the general introduction of the process should rest on a 'well planned and well directed pilot project' (ACAS, 1986). (See Delany)

In the light of these recommendations, the DES funded the 1987–9 School Teacher Appraisal Pilot Study. Funds were made available through educational support grants for the piloting of teacher and headteacher appraisal in six LEAs – Croydon, Cumbria, Newcastle, Salford, Somerset and Suffolk. Some 150 schools of all types took part and by the end of the project almost 1700 teachers and 200 headteachers had been appraised. The project was co-ordinated at local level by LEA co-ordination teams and at national level by a team from the National Development Centre for School Management Training (NDC–SMT) directed by Ray Bolam. The pilot study was evaluated by a team from the Cambridge Institute of Education (CIE), directed by Howard Bradley.

Those involved in the pilot study reported to the successor of the ACAS Appraisal/Training Working Group, the National Steering Group (NSG). The NSG drew on the pilot study experience in making a series of recommendations (NSG, 1989) to the Secretary of State for Education and Science on the principles and processes of a national appraisal framework.

The central NSG recommendation was that an appraisal framework for teachers in England and Wales should be established in the spirit of the principles set out in the ACAS report. The model of appraisal reflected concerns with the professional development of teachers and the good professional management of schools.

The suggestion of the NSG was for those on teachers' and headteachers' conditions of service, with the exception of probationers, and licensed and articled teachers, to be appraised when systematically and continuously on a two-yearly basis. Teachers would be appraised by their headteacher or someone else either with a management responsibility for them or seen as at HO by credible and experienced. Headteachers would be appraised by two appraisers – one, at least, with appropriate headship experience and the other an LEA officer. A key responsibility for the training, monitoring and support of the scheme would be given to LEAs. The approach would ensure that everyone would be appraised consistently within the appraisal framework set out, a framework designed to provide common purposes, principles, stages and frequency. It is, however, a framework which leaves flexibility for planning and development at school and LEA level (see Appendix 1).

The NSG report forms an important basis for the present (October 1989 to April 1990) period of consultation about the introduction of a national appraisal scheme. Introduced?

3

THE PURPOSES OF APPRAISAL

Appraisal comes to the education system with a good deal of attendant baggage. Evidence from North American school experience, lessons from other occupations, feelings towards appraisal generated by previous home-produced schemes and by official statements about appraisal, have all had an impact. In addition, appraisal has to find a place among a number of current initiatives designed to improve the quality of education.

Appraisal is, of course, a particularly sensitive initiative. In part this reflects the way it has at times been presented; for example, as a device for 'weeding out weak teachers' or a means of assessing suitability for 'merit pay'. The sensitivity also reflects the focus of appraisal, which is concerned with matters of professional and career development and goes to the heart of the teacher's work. In part the sensitivity relates to it being yet another initiative which can break down traditional classroom isolation. Bearing in mind these sensitivities and the variety of potential uses possible for appraisal, it is important to be clear about the purposes appraisal is supposed to accomplish.

In the most basic sense, appraisal can be defined narrowly as 'the forming of qualitative judgments' (DES, 1983). Such a definition raises a number of issues, drawing attention to the need to consider the criteria on which judgements are made and the purposes of making them in the first place. Typically appraisal involves an analysis of past performance with the aim of planning for the future. The question to be addressed here is 'to what end?'

A number of North American writers on appraisal in particular, have distinguished between contrasting purposes in appraisal.

Wise *et al.* (1985) provide the framework shown in Figure 1.1, which depicts the varied possible purposes of appraisal. They see appraisal as operating at both individual and organizational levels.

Purpose / Level	Improvement	Accountability
Individual	Individual staff development	Individual personnel decisions e.g. job status
Organizational	School improvement	School status decisions (e.g. accreditation)

Figure 1.1 *A framework for understanding appraisal*
Source: Wise *et al.* (1985). © University of Chicago Press, 1985. Reproduced with permission.

They argue that in practice appraisal schemes often serve more than one purpose 'our case studies reinforce the conclusion that a single teacher evaluation process can serve only one goal well' (Wise *et al.*, 1985, p. 106). Their table provides a useful index for organizing the literature on appraisal. Particularly useful is the way it draws attention to the fact that appraisal has an impact at the level of both the individual teacher and the school. Figure 1.1 also makes the common distinction between appraisal for development or improvement purposes and appraisal for the sake of accountability.

In similar vein, Wise and Darling-Hammond (1984) offer an alternative contrast between bureaucratic and professional appraisal or, to use the preferred North American term, evaluation.

> In the bureaucratic conception, the district (1) relies primarily on administrators to design and operate a uniform teacher evaluation process, (2) bases evaluation on generalised criteria like generic teaching skills or other context-free teaching behaviours, (3) recognises a fixed set of learning outcomes, and (4) treats all teachers alike. Bureaucratic evaluation is highly standardised. It is procedurally oriented and organised by checklist. It is designed to monitor conformance with routines.
>
> In the professional conception, the district (1) involves teachers in the development and operation of the teacher evaluation process, (2) bases evaluation on professional standards of practice that are client-oriented, (3) recognises multiple teaching strategies and learning outcomes, and (4) treats teachers differently according to their teaching assignments, stages of development, and classroom goals. Professional evaluation is clinical, practice-oriented, and analytic. It is designed to assess the appropriateness of strategies and decisions.
>
> (Wise and Darling-Hammond, 1984, p. 30)

Yet another common distinction in North American writing is that made between formative and summative evaluation. Broadly speaking, formative appraisal or evaluation corresponds to Wise *et al*'s appraisal for 'improvement', whereas summative evaluation leans towards purposes of 'accountability'. Formative appraisal is concerned with helping teachers develop as opposed to simply judging where they are at a given point in time.

It has, in fact, become relatively common in North America to supplement traditional summative schemes with more developmental and formative ones. Where such schemes operate side by side a clear distinction is made. These trends reflect recent North American moves away from linking appraisal largely with questions of qualification and tenure, and show an increasing concern for professional development and growth. A recent analysis of these trends points to the thinking responsible for them: 'assessment to ascertain degree of competence needs to be separated from evaluation to help teachers stay vital and dynamic' (Association of Teacher Educators, 1988, p. 42).

The trend towards support for appraisal as a means of development or improvement can also be seen in a recent paper by McLaughlin. Noting that traditional approaches to appraisal have often been seen as 'a waste of time and resources', McLaughlin argues the merits of a developmental model. In particular she draws attention to four key factors built upon by such a model:

> teacher motivation and sense of efficacy;
> effective communication and shared goals;
> principals' instructional leadership;
> teacher learning and development.
>
> (McLaughlin, 1986, p. 164)

The argument is that teachers are far more likely to improve if they are provided with informed feedback and opportunities to communicate effectively about their work than if they are made to go through an 'uneven, desultory ritual' or a 'standard checklist' approach (McLaughlin, 1986). In other words the contemporary advice from North America is to go for a developmental appraisal system.

It is interesting to move from these examples of North American thinking to the <u>British context</u>. In the ACAS report, appraisal was seen as serving a number of developmental purposes. These are embodied in the widely quoted 'ACAS principles':

i. Planning the induction of EG [entry-grade] teachers and assessing their fitness to transfer to an MPG [main professional grade].

ii. Planning the participation of individual teachers in in-service training.

iii. Helping individual teachers, their headteachers and their employers to see when a new or modified assignment would help the professional development of individual teachers and improve their career prospects.

iv. Identifying the potential of teachers for career development, with an eye to their being helped by appropriate in-service training.

v. Recognition of teachers experiencing performance difficulty the purpose being to provide help through appropriate guidance, counselling and training. Disciplinary procedures would remain quite separate, but might need to draw on relevant information from the appraisal records.

vi. Staff appointment procedures. The relevant elements of appraisal should be available to better inform those charged with the responsibility for providing references.

(ACAS, 1986, p. 2)

The working group took the view that appraisal should not be seen

> as a series of perfunctory periodic events, <u>but as a continuous and systematic process intended to help individual teachers with their professional development and career planning, and to help ensure that the in-service training and deployment of teachers matches the complementary needs of individual teachers and the schools</u>. . . . It will be seen that what the Working Group has in mind is a positive process, intended to raise the quality of education in schools by providing teachers with better job satisfaction, more appropriate in-service training and better planned career development based upon more informed decisions.

(ACAS, 1986, pp. 2–3)

With the exception of the use of appraisal in connection with the probationary year, all the other principles outlined in the ACAS report have gone through from the School Teacher Appraisal Pilot Study as principles held as important in the national appraisal framework recommended by the National Steering Group.

An amplification of the set of purposes given in the ACAS report is provided by the list of <u>possible outcomes of appraisal included in the Cambridge Institute of Education survey questionnaire</u>, issued to samples of teachers in the six pilot LEAs in Spring 1989.

(a) Identification of your INSET needs

(b) A new or modified role

(c) The development of professional relationships within the school in which you work

(d) The promotion of consistency between your aims and those of the school

(e) Enabling you to express views about the school in the expectation that they will receive serious consideration

(f) Identifying your potential for career development

(g) Identifying and helping with any performance difficulty you may have had

(h) Obtaining candid feedback on your past performance, and gaining reassurance and motivation for the future

(i) Promoting the development of your school

(j) Improving the performance of your pupils

(k) Contributing to your reference

(l) Enabling you to develop further your expertise/skills

While varying proportions of those surveyed had actually experienced the above outcomes to a significant extent, all outcomes were seen to some degree in the School Teacher Appraisal Pilot Study. This demonstrates the wide range of outcomes possible from a supportive and constructive appraisal scheme. In particular, appraisal appeared an important means of improving communication within schools and of providing individual teachers with feedback, reassurance and motivation. Individuals appear to emerge from the process with a clearer sense of purpose and direction and there was evidence to suggest it had led to improvements in the performance of both teachers and their pupils.

These potential gains offer encouragement to those concerned about the time and cost implications of appraisal. They show that the investment of time and energy in appraisal can pay handsome dividends. The model of appraisal trialled in the pilot study was concerned above all with the professional development of teachers. It was this emphasis and the concern to carry through this philosophy at all stages of training and of the process itself that lay behind the improvements referred to. What was achieved was a fresh and vital process, time-consuming yet rewarding. What was avoided was the bureaucratic ritual so often lamented in North American writing.

KEY PRINCIPLES IN APPRAISAL

Appraisal schemes can therefore be operated in a variety of ways. There are, however, certain key principles which have emerged from experience as relevant to a developmental approach to appraisal. These can be useful in pointing to how appraisal can most successfully be carried out in the interests of enhancing the development of both the school and the individual teacher.

A pre-pilot study assessment of the features of a good appraisal scheme was given in Britain by Nuttall (1986). He lists nine such features, which can be summarized as follows:

1 Experience with institutional self-evaluation and constructive self-criticism facilitates appraisal.

2 Effective appraisal schemes cannot serve formative and summative purposes simultaneously.

3 A good scheme must link the results of appraisal to appropriate action.

4   The importance of involving those who will be appraised in the process. At one level, this means involving them in the development of any scheme, rather than imposing it upon them. At a deeper level, it means ensuring that self-appraisal is an important component (if it cannot be the only component for reasons of credibility or comparability).

5   A good scheme must give the teacher some autonomy.

6   A shared understanding of both criteria and processes among all parties is essential, which also means that there must be a clear understanding of the role each party plays.

7   Schemes which employ more than one observer or appraiser gain reliability and validity, as well as credibility, particularly if peers are involved as well as superiors.

8   Research in industry has shown the value of using ipsative rating scales, that is, scales that ask raters to compare the performance of the individual on one dimension with his or her performance on the other dimensions to indicate relative strengths and weaknesses.

9   None of these desirable qualities can be realized without adequate training. Training must embrace not only particular skills (such as those of observation, interviewing and counselling), but also more general managerial skills and a discussion of values and assumptions.

These points tie in with advice on the successful introduction of appraisal emerging from other sources. They point to the need for care to be taken over developing a suitable climate for appraisal and for involving those affected in the implementation of the scheme. The advice given is similar to that emerging both from the School Teacher Appraisal Pilot Study and from many North American sources.

For example, Conley (1987), in a review of appraisal literature from the North American perspective, identifies a series of eight critical attributes of effective evaluation systems:

1   All participants accept the validity of the system.

2   All participants thoroughly understand the mechanics of the system.

3   Evaluatees know that the performance criteria have a clear consistent rationale.

4   Evaluators are properly trained in the procedural and substantive use of the system.

5   Levels of evaluation are employed, each with a different goal.

6   The evaluation distinguishes between the formative and summative dimensions.

7   A variety of evaluation methods are used.

8   Evaluation is a district priority.

There is a surprising degree of unanimity in these and other North American sources and many of the points made have stood up well in the British context.

The School Teacher Appraisal Pilot Study took the principles and purposes already referred to in the ACAS report as its starting point. Appraisal was seen as a continuous, positive, systematic and cyclical process. The basic recommendations of the ACAS report were developed within the six pilot LEAs, as the following examples show. Salford LEA saw appraisal as needing to:

- be continuous and systematic. Because it is structured and cyclical it regularises review and development

- be conducted by fellow-professionals who understand the nature of the job and the context in which the individual works

- be responsive to the specific needs of individual schools. Teachers should help to formulate these procedures and they should be known to, and understood by, all

- have documentation, access to it and the use made of it, agreed

- be separate from LEA incapability procedures.

(Salford LEA, 1988a, p. 6)

Somerset LEA stressed that its appraisal scheme was 'formative, consultative, developmental and supportive' (Somerset LEA, 1988a).

The following recommendations for a successful appraisal interview from Suffolk LEA can be seen as typical of the principles applied in the pilot study to all stages of the process and to the process as a whole:

To be really effective, a dialogue must attempt, as far as is possible, to satisfy a number of basic criteria. The process should try to make the appraisal dialogue:

Objective: by removing prejudice, subjective/unsubstantiated comment, and personality clashes.

Honest: by giving the teacher an accurate picture of where he/she stands.

Constructive: by building on strengths and past achievements in order to agree targets for improvement and development.

Valid: by justifying all points of constructive criticism with facts and examples.

Two Way: by giving an opportunity for listening and talking by both parties.

Developmental: by achieving a joint review and problem-solving approach.

Effective: by translating into a plan, with targets and dates, the outcome of the discussion.

Realistic: by ensuring that achievable targets are mutually agreed.

Encouraging: by praising past performance and reinforcing the idea that further training and development can only add to job satisfaction and motivation.

(Suffolk LEA, 1988a, p. 15)

Taking these findings as a whole we conclude that key principles in appraisal are:

1   the need for commitment to the process and credibility in those presenting and introducing the scheme;

9

2 the need to consult with and involve all interested parties in planning for appraisal;

3 the need for the scheme to be developmental, constructive and positive;

4 the need to provide adequate training for those involved in appraisal;

5 the need actively to involve teachers not only in the design of the process but also in discussing criteria used and the areas chosen for appraisal;

6 the need for the process to be two-way and related to the individual school context and the appraisee's own stage of development.

THE APPRAISAL PROCESS

The rest of this book is concerned with a consideration of the various stages of the appraisal process. It relates to the model of appraisal found during the School Teacher Appraisal Pilot Study (see Figure 1.2). We explain the stages in more detail in subsequent chapters; here we confine ourselves to a few general points.

The process described here is a cyclical and continuous one. Essentially it is divided into three stages: preparation, interview and follow-up.

Preparation

Some of the more general preparation for appraisal involves awareness-raising and training both inside and outside the school. Once the appraisal process starts for each individual, the aim of preparation is to ensure that both appraiser and appraisee come to the interview able to hold a discussion of substance and to avoid ill-informed comments. The preparation phase includes an initial meeting to set up the process and a range of approaches to gathering data on the teacher's performance, including classroom observation. In order to ensure that the process promotes reflection, it has typically included self-appraisal.

This in turn ensures that the appraisee comes to the interview with a clear view of what to raise. The aim, therefore, is that preparation is systematic and relates to agreed areas across the full range of the teacher's job. In the case of headteacher appraisal, where appraisers come from outside the school, it is preceded by a period of 'familiarization', designed to acquaint the appraisers with the context of the head's job. In two of the pilot study LEAs in particular the process was also preceded by a process of whole-school review in order to create a context or backdrop for individual appraisal. We consider preparation for appraisal in more detail in Chapter 2 and in view of the prominence it has attracted we consider classroom observation separately in Chapter 3. We consider training for appraisal in Chapter 7 and headteacher appraisal in Chapter 6.

The Interview

Central to the process is the interview. This can be seen as a chance for uninterrupted and sustained discussion of past performance and future plans. Typically it encompasses a review of successes, areas for development and constraints and leads to target setting related to the present job, as well as to general professional career development. It results in an agreed summary/action plan or statement. We consider the appraisal interview in greater detail in Chapter 4.

fund in pilot study

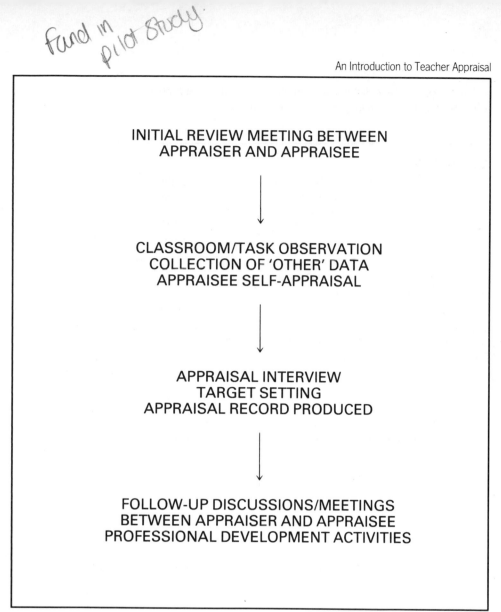

INITIAL REVIEW MEETING BETWEEN
APPRAISER AND APPRAISEE

CLASSROOM/TASK OBSERVATION
COLLECTION OF 'OTHER' DATA
APPRAISEE SELF-APPRAISAL

APPRAISAL INTERVIEW
TARGET SETTING
APPRAISAL RECORD PRODUCED

FOLLOW-UP DISCUSSIONS/MEETINGS
BETWEEN APPRAISER AND APPRAISEE
PROFESSIONAL DEVELOPMENT ACTIVITIES

Figure 1.2   *Components in the appraisal process*

Follow-Up

Crucial to the whole process is the follow-up stage; indeed the credibility of appraisal depends on success here. At this stage targets are worked on, supported and monitored.

At the end of the School Teacher Appraisal Pilot Study, the NSG recommended that the appraisal process should be a two-year programme of activity, with the preparation phase taking about half a term of the period available for teachers and slightly longer for head-teachers. In essence, therefore, much of the two years is spent on follow-up work in the form of professional development activities arising from the review process. However, it should be noted that the School Teacher Appraisal Pilot Study experience showed that the preparation and interview stages are themselves developmental, leading, for example, to increased reflection, improved motivation and better communication. Appraisal can therefore be both a form of staff development in itself and a means of securing further development. We consider the links

11

between appraisal and development in Chapter 5 and look at how the links can be strengthened through the effective management of appraisal at LEA and school level in Chapter 8.

SUMMARY

The range of purposes noted in this section indicates the scope of a developmental model of appraisal. Potentially, this model of appraisal can lead to wide-ranging improvements. The process can serve as a spur to reflection or can boost morale, through providing a chance for praise and recognition. It can lead to a better understanding of an individual's INSET and development needs in the broadest sense and can provide a means of reconciling an individual's aims with those of the school. The process serves as an opportunity for reviewing progress and acts as an incentive to clarify thinking on future plans, including in the area of career planning. Above all it provides a means of improving communication and teamwork within a school and of giving the school a greater sense of cohesion and direction.

What follows is an attempt to indicate how these benefits can be achieved. We do not, however, rest our argument solely on the need to carry out appraisal in a developmental way. We see a major task over the next few years as the need to integrate appraisal and other current initiatives. We feel that the developmental potential of appraisal can be strengthened by linking it with school development planning and management development. Providing each has the prime aim of increasing the professionalism of teachers, then real improvements can result. What might be achieved is outlined in the aspirations towards appraisal of one deputy head:

> improved professionalism means agreed aims and objectives, a set pattern of values and attitudes, clear guidelines, strong commitment, best use of expertise, resources and plant, trust among staff, improved curriculum and therefore better standards of work from children.
>
> (Bradley *et al.*, 1988)

Chapter 2

Preparing for Appraisal

As became apparent in the previous chapter, appraisal is more than simply classroom observation or the appraisal interview. Indeed, to have the positive impact we wish for it, for both the individual teacher and the school, appraisal has to be embedded into the rhythm of the school. It needs to be linked to other activities and strategies that are part of, or become part of, the school's day-to-day routine. From this perspective classroom observation and the appraisal interview are, as it were, sandwiched between sets of other activities that support these core elements of the appraisal process, and link them to the school's other routine and developmental activities. These two sets of activities that bound observation and interview can be broadly classified as preparatory and developmental.

This chapter is concerned with the preparatory activities. We have grouped these into four: climate setting and readiness; whole-school review; the establishing of criteria; and other forms of data gathering apart from classroom observation. In common with the other chapters in this book, this chapter discusses these activities from two perspectives: first what we know from the literature on, and experience of, appraisal in general; and second what we have learned from our evaluation of the School Teacher Appraisal Pilot Study. The contrast between the 'ideal' models and the 'reality' of implementing an appraisal scheme is particularly illuminating. In the final section of the chapter we draw the discussion together into a series of action-oriented key points.

PREPARATION AND CLIMATE SETTING

The literature concerned with change in education, although unanimous on the importance of preparation and climate setting, is reticent in suggesting strategies for bringing these about. We do, however, have some knowledge of the characteristics of an effective system for appraisal. Describing these characteristics and thereby suggesting an ideal model is a first step in eliciting strategies that will move us towards that goal.

There have been two major studies of appraisal (or teacher evaluation) recently carried out by the 'Research for Better Schools' and Rand organizations in the United States of America. Their conclusions on the characteristics of effective appraisal systems are worth quoting.

First, Research for Better Schools: their findings (*vide* Buttram and Wilson, 1987) suggest that progressive school districts are:

- linking evaluation systems to research on effective teacher practices;

- providing improved training for evaluators;

- holding administrators more accountable for conducting evaluations;

- using evaluation-identified teacher deficiencies to focus staff development; and

13

- making teachers active partners in the evaluation process.

The Rand corporation study on effective practices in teacher evaluation draws similar conclusions from its research (Wise *et al.*, 1985):

> Conclusion 1: To succeed, a teacher evaluation system must suit the educational goals, management style, conception of teaching, and community values of the school district.
>
> Conclusion 2: Top-level commitment to and resources for evaluation outweigh checklists and procedures.
>
> Conclusion 3: The school district must decide the main purpose of its teacher evaluation system and then match the process to the purpose.
>
> Conclusion 4: To sustain resource commitments and political support, teacher evaluation must be seen to have utility, which in turn depends on the efficient use of resources to achieve reliability, validity, and cost-effectiveness.
>
> Conclusion 5: Teacher involvement and responsibility improve the quality of teacher evaluation.

Two further American studies (quoted in Wise *et al.*, 1985) are also helpful in illuminating the ideal type of climate in which to conduct appraisal.

A review by Fuller *et al.* (1982), of the research on individual effectiveness within the context of organizations, suggests that with respect to teacher evaluation both individual and organizational benefits will result from: (1) agreement between teachers and senior management in accepting the goals and means for appraisal; (2) increased communication between teachers and senior management; (3) lower prescriptiveness of work tasks; (4) teachers' perceptions that evaluation is soundly based; and (5) teacher input into the production of a diversity of evaluation criteria.

These findings agree with those of Natriello and Dornbusch (1980–1) on the reasons for teacher satisfaction with appraisal systems. They found teacher satisfaction strongly related to (a) perceptions that all appraisers and appraisees share the same criteria for evaluation; (b) frequent sampling of teacher performance; (c) more frequent communication and feedback; and (d) the teachers' ability to help define the criteria for appraisal. Interestingly, frequency of negative feedback did not cause dissatisfaction, but infrequency of evaluation did.

These findings suggest that teacher satisfaction with appraisal systems seems to rest on the perception that the process is soundly based, that it is relatively frequent, collaborative and developmental, and that the teacher has some control over the setting of criteria and the major elements of the process. These studies, together with Nuttall's list of qualities of a 'good' appraisal scheme (Chapter 1, pp. 7–8) present a fairly complete and optimistic overview of the conditions necessary for effective appraisal. These conditions also act as criteria against which readiness for appraisal can be assessed.

Schools are not the same; each approaches innovation from a different perspective and this also has to be taken into account when preparing for appraisal. We have already discussed some responses to the question: 'What are the necessary pre-conditions for a successful appraisal scheme?' This is not quite the same question as: 'What predisposes schools towards readiness for appraisal?' This question has more to do with the internal character or the organizational culture of a school than with appraisal *per se*. This is a very complex issue. It is generally agreed however that factors such as a concensus about the aims of the school, a high degree of collaboration, a relatively stable environment, ongoing staff development, strong leadership at all levels, and an emphasis on planning, are significantly related to a school's capacity to handle change and innovation.

The following questions for assessing the school's general readiness for innovation may provide some help in assessing this elusive quality. They are adapted from *The Handbook of Organisation Development in Schools* (Schmuck and Runkel 1985, Chapter 9):

1 Is there a 'critical mass' (significant minority) of staff prepared to support the change?

2 Is there high staff turnover?

3 Are there resources and is there support?

4 Does the school climate support collaboration?

5 If so, do staff possess the skills required for collaborative group work?

6 Is there a spirit of risk-taking in the school?

Obviously a high score is not required on each item, but an above-average positive score across the six questions would normally be regarded as a good indication of readiness. If this is not the case, time should be spent either before starting appraisal or during its early stages to develop sufficient 'readiness' within the school.

WHOLE-SCHOOL REVIEW

Another strategy for preparing for appraisal is to precede the introduction of an appraisal scheme by some form of school review or self-evaluation. This strategy fulfils three purposes: First, it provides a context for appraisal – it is far less threatening to individual teachers if the school has been 'appraised' first, and they can then set their own appraisal within that context. Second, such activities can assist in developing 'readiness'. Third, linking whole-school review to teacher appraisal results in a much more powerful strategy for school improvement. The implicit argument is that if appraisal is viewed as a developmental rather than an accountability exercise, and if the individual teacher is appraised within the context of the school, then school improvement is an inevitable outcome of appraisal.

In the School Teacher Appraisal Pilot Study the working paper produced by the Cumbria working party (1988) was explicit about the ultimate purpose of their appraisal scheme and provides a useful rationale for linking appraisal to whole-school review:

> The Working Party which has produced this policy statement recognises that the professional development of teachers is most effective if it builds upon appraisal. There is also a recognition that effective professional development can only take place in parallel with institutional development. Professional development entails curriculum, and total institutional development.
>
> A fundamental premise requiring emphasis is the fact that teaching staff appraisal and whole school self-evaluation are closely interlinked and complementary. Teachers' professional development based upon appraisal will be most effective if it takes place in tandem with curricular and organisational review, development, and self-evaluation of the whole school. Regular staff appraisal provides a structure within which teachers are allowed to develop their talents to the full within the organisation as a whole in addition to enabling them to improve in areas of weakness. Individual teacher appraisal and whole school self-evaluation both identify in-service education needs.
>
> More specifically, the establishment of effective individual teacher appraisal, together with the organisation's systematic self-evaluation, demands a

great deal of schools and colleges. Both identify INSET needs. Basic rethinking of what INSET is all about is required. The structures, systems and procedures within schools/colleges need to ensure that each teacher has an opportunity to make an input into the discussion of the INSET needs of the school/college and the teachers in it at that point in time; the LEA has a responsibility to meet those needs.

This approach to the linking of school-based review to teacher appraisal is well summarized in Figure 2.1. It is interesting to note that many schools in the Cumbria LEA have had experience of GRIDS (Guidelines for the Review and Internal Development of Schools) and have been heavily influenced by it as a means of school improvement and staff development.

CRITERIA IN APPRAISAL

At some stage in any appraisal process the question of criteria will inevitably arise. At its simplest level this question concerns the basis on which judgements of good practice are made or targets are judged to have been met. Often the issue of criteria is not tackled until late in the appraisal process. Our experience suggests that this tends to lead to an uncritical approach to appraisal, which in the end does no one any good. Concentrating on the issue of criteria during the preparation phase, however, provides a focus for the appraisal activity, involves teachers in the process early on, thus enhancing ownership, and ensures that from its inception the appraisal process has some critical edge to it.

The criteria used in making such judgements can be arrived at in a variety of ways. Research on teacher effectiveness may be referred to in order to construct a model of good teaching, against which teachers are compared. In this approach, the model would draw on conclusions drawn from a vast range of research on the practice of teaching. Another approach lies in making use of the lessons of psychology in general and of learning theory in particular. These lessons constitute a set of principles, which can guide good practice. Their presence or absence in a particular lesson might be used to explain its success or failure. Criteria for appraisal might be based on experience and take the form of a personal or shared view of what constitutes good practice. Such a view would typically be formed within a school. Criteria for appraisal might also come from individual, school, LEA or national objectives or some combination of these. We should emphasize that these different approaches, which will now be discussed in a little more detail, are not necessarily mutually exclusive.

Criteria Derived from the Research on Teaching

There is a good deal of literature, particularly from North America, concerned with teacher effectiveness. It is possible to use recommendations from this as the basis of criteria for appraising teachers. Figure 2.2 provides a useful approach to considering the teacher effectiveness research; it illustrates the factors identified by the research into teacher effectiveness. These areas indicate possible categories for classifying criteria when developing them for an appraisal scheme.

Teacher effectiveness research utilizes a 'process–product' design. On the basis of observation, attempts are made to identify relationships between the teaching process and certain student outcomes such as gains in test scores. This approach has led to the 'direct instruction' model of learning in which the concept of engaged academic learning time (i.e. the time pupils actually spend actively on task) is held to be critical.

Doyle's (1987) authoritative summary of this model is as follows:

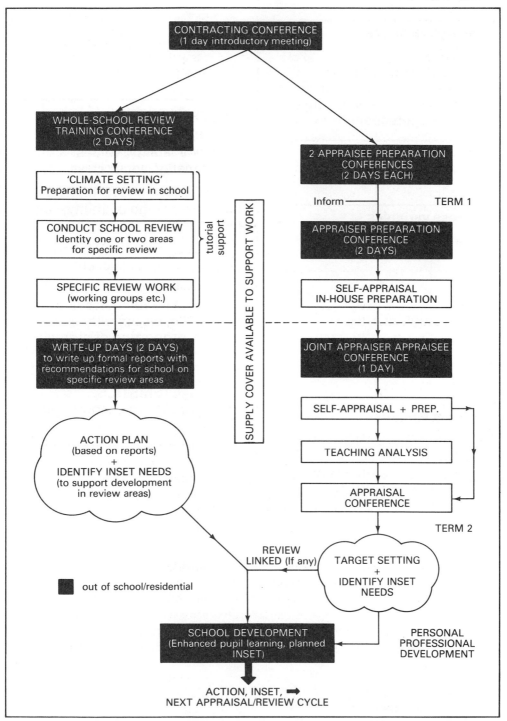

Figure 2.1 *The Cumbria LEA approach to teacher appraisal that utilizes SBR: sequence of review and appraisal in pilot study schools*
Source: Cumbria LEA (1988)

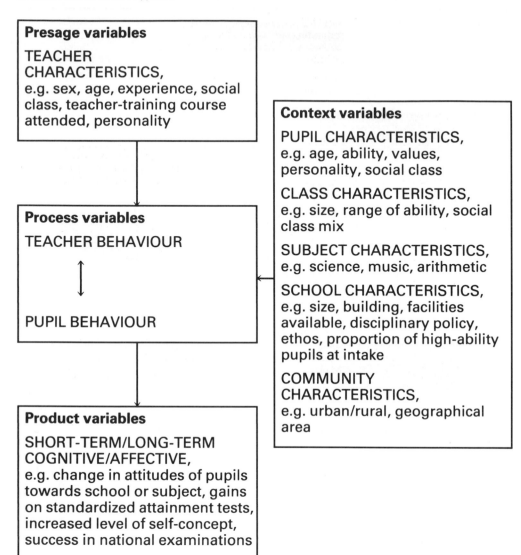

Presage variables

TEACHER CHARACTERISTICS, e.g. sex, age, experience, social class, teacher-training course attended, personality

Process variables

TEACHER BEHAVIOUR

↑
↓

PUPIL BEHAVIOUR

Product variables

SHORT-TERM/LONG-TERM COGNITIVE/AFFECTIVE, e.g. change in attitudes of pupils towards school or subject, gains on standardized attainment tests, increased level of self-concept, success in national examinations

Context variables

PUPIL CHARACTERISTICS, e.g. age, ability, values, personality, social class

CLASS CHARACTERISTICS, e.g. size, range of ability, social class mix

SUBJECT CHARACTERISTICS, e.g. science, music, arithmetic

SCHOOL CHARACTERISTICS, e.g. size, building, facilities available, disciplinary policy, ethos, proportion of high-ability pupils at intake

COMMUNITY CHARACTERISTICS, e.g. urban/rural, geographical area

Figure 2.2 *Factors involved in research into teacher effectiveness*
Source: Kyriacou and Newson (1982)

Classroom studies of teaching effects have generally supported a direct and structured approach to instruction (Brophy and Good, 1986). That is, students usually achieve more when a teacher:

1 Emphasizes academic goals, makes them explicit, and expects students to be able to master the curriculum;

2 Carefully organizes and sequences curriculum experiences;

3 Clearly explains and illustrates what students are to learn;

4 Frequently asks direct and specific questions to monitor students' progress and check their understanding;

5 Provides students with ample opportunity to practise, gives prompts and feedback to ensure success and correct mistakes, and allows students to practise a skill until it is overlearned and automatic;

6 Reviews regularly and holds students accountable for work.

From this perspective, a teacher promotes student learning by being active in planning and organizing instruction, explaining to students what they are to learn, arranging occasions for guided practice, monitoring progress, providing feedback, and otherwise helping students understand and accomplish work.

Unfortunately as Doyle (1987, p. 96) points out, 'little attention is given in process–product studies as to how observed conditions of effective teaching are established in classrooms or how teachers acquire teaching abilities'. Basic issues of staff development therefore lie outside this research tradition. But Doyle continues to suggest two ways in which this research can be 'translated' into a form useful for staff development and also appraisal. He suggests:

> two approaches to staff development that represent substantially different translations of research on teaching effects. In the first approach, research findings are seen as sources of guidelines for teaching that teachers can apply directly in their classrooms. In the second approach, findings are viewed as sources of analytical categories teachers can use to reason about their teaching and construct solutions to classroom problems.
>
> (Doyle, 1987, p. 96)

There are other examples in North America of ways in which teacher effectiveness research has been used in appraisal systems. Some schemes have mainly been based on an analysis of teacher effectiveness research, with the emphasis on translating the research into a series of performance indicators that can be rated. *Domains of the Florida Performance Measurement System* (Office of Teacher Education, 1983) is a comprehensive and closely argued example of this approach. Materials from Greenwich, Connecticut provide another illustration of how an analysis of teacher effectiveness research can produce criteria for teacher appraisal. The 'summary of effective teaching practices' (as seen in Figure 2.3) gives a feel for this approach.

For our purposes, however, there are certain limitations to the teacher effectiveness research; much of it comes from North America and reflects their educational culture; most of the research has been undertaken in reading and maths classes of elementary grade pupils; and the 'product' is usually standardized test scores. Taken as a whole, the effective teaching research has not yet produced an agreed and sufficiently comprehensive and generally accepted characterization of teaching, but it remains a useful source of ideas.

Another approach to enhancing teacher effectiveness through appraisal is to use the various 'models of teaching' as a basis for setting criteria. In their classic text *Models of Teaching* (1986) Bruce Joyce and Marsha Weil argue passionately that teachers need to acquire a repertoire of teaching models which they can then apply to varying teaching objectives, content areas and types of student. They argue that:

> There are many powerful models of teaching designed to bring about particular kinds of learning and to help students become more effective learners. As

19

I. GENERAL ATTITUDE

The effective teacher has a strong sense of efficacy.

- Has realistically high expectations for each student's behavior and achievement
- Expects students to be successful
- Takes responsibility for what happens in the classroom and for the students' learning

II. STUDENTS' AFFECTIVE DEVELOPMENT

The effective teacher fosters the development of a positive self-concept in each student.

- Is courteous to students and promotes courtesy among students
- Shows respect for students' ideas and feelings
- Gives praise which is specific and is perceived as genuine
- Avoids sarcasm and personal criticism
- Helps students develop a sense of responsibility for their own learning and behavior

III. CLASSROOM MANAGEMENT

The effective teacher manages the classroom so that maximum time is available for teaching and learning.

- Establishes classroom routines at the beginning of the year and makes certain that students know those routines

IV. INSTRUCTION

The effective teacher organizes instruction to actively involve all students in their own learning.

- Selects objectives that are appropriate, both in sequence (order of instruction, concepts, skills, etc.) and in developmental level
- Selects teaching strategies that are appropriate
- Demonstrates a good grasp of the subject matter
- Presents material clearly
- Checks for comprehension as the lesson progresses; appraises teaching strategy in light of students' comprehension and changes strategy if necessary
- Gives feedback which lets students know what they have learned and what they still need to know
- Uses guiding and probing questions when students don't know answers
- Develops students' abilities to think on higher cognitive levels
- Involves all students in class activities
- Monitors the individual student's progress

Figure 2.3   *Summary of effective teaching practices*
Source: Greenwich, Connecticut, Committee on Effective Teaching (1983)

educators we need to identify these models and to select the ones that we will monitor in order to develop and increase our own effectiveness.

(Joyce and Weil, 1986, p. 1)

In their book they identify and describe in detail some 20 teaching models divided into four families: the information processing, the personal, the social and the behavioural systems families. They also describe the application of the models to various educational objectives and a range of strategies for acquiring them.

Taken together these models provide a more holistic approach to teaching than the research on teaching effects, and as such provide another basis for establishing criteria for appraisal in schools.

Criteria Drawn from Psychology

It is, of course, possible to base appraisal on constructs gained from sources other than the teacher effectiveness or 'models of teaching' approaches. For example the starting points may be a knowledge of psychology in general and of learning and motivation theories in particular. Kyriacou (1986) offers the model shown in Figure 2.4, which illustrates some of the concepts used in this approach.

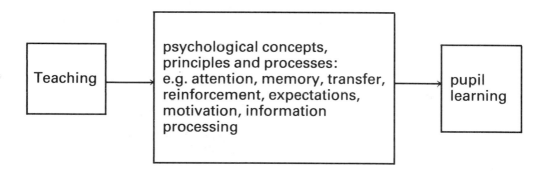

Figure 2.4   *Psychological level of analysis*
Source: Kyriacou (1986)

Kyriacou sees this approach as going beneath the surface level of analysis, as exemplified by the teacher effectiveness research, to explore the underlying psychological factors at work in a classroom.

Ideas for basing appraisal on the lessons from psychology can be gleaned from the work of Madeline Hunter in the USA (in Hosford, 1984) and Diane Montgomery (1984) in the UK. Hunter's influence is ubiquitous; a well-known example (see Figure 2.5) is found in the approach developed in Pittsburgh, where a model for teaching and evaluation called PRISM was developed, based on her ideas (see Wallace, in Hopkins, 1987). Montgomery's approach, which again relies on principles such as attention span, reinforcement and positive feedback, is illustrated in her description of a project carried out in schools and designed to improve the performance of young teachers through classroom observation. She stresses the importance of the 'tactical planning' of lessons, an approach which 'involves activity change based upon the attention span of the class'. Her argument is that 'if lessons are analysed in terms of tactics it is possible to demonstrate the points at which the lesson will deteriorate or has deteriorated and why' (1984, pp. 28–9).

These approaches based on psychology present an alternative route to using teacher effectiveness research for deriving criteria in appraisal. Here teachers would be appraised according to their application of 'proven psychological principles'.

Some criticisms of this approach should, however, be noted. In particular, it has been criticized for being too instrumental, for not allowing teachers or pupils sufficient control over their own teaching and learning, and for not producing long-lasting results. There has been some reaction to such an approach as being too scientific, particularly from those who see teaching as an art or a craft (Hosford, 1984). Similarly, it may be felt that the approach underplays the role of lesson content. It is also worth noting that many of the so-called 'proven psychological principles' were demonstrated in clinical or laboratory conditions rather than in the classroom.

Criteria Drawn from Experience

A third way of arriving at criteria for appraisal is to devise a list of teaching skills felt to be effective by those involved in the appraisal process and based on their own experience. Such a list might be called a practitioner's view of effective teaching. Kyriacou's (1986) model illustrating this approach is shown in Figure 2.6. It rests on the views of experienced teachers, having 'emerged largely from the perspective of effective teaching employed by teacher educators' (1986, p. 29). It might serve, however, as a useful framework for those in schools or LEAs involved in developing appraisal criteria.

The following list of characteristics associated with good teaching was drawn up for us by a group of experienced teachers. It is interesting to compare these with the characteristics derived from teacher effectiveness research or other sources:

- ability to communicate clearly;
- ability to form relationships with pupils appropriate to the learning task;
- control of class;
- variety of approach;
- good planning;
- suitable appropriate use of resources;
- self-critical approach leading to adaptation;
- degree of pupil involvement;
- overall purpose of lesson – has useful learning taken place?;
- sensitivity to individual pupils' needs.

Criteria Based on Goals, Targets or Objectives

It is possible to make use of any of the three previous approaches when formulating criteria for appraisal; it is also possible to combine them. We now move on to consider what might be called mechanisms for formulating criteria and for incorporating them into the appraisal process.

One possible mechanism for formulating appraisal criteria for individuals lies in the outcomes of school-based review exercises and school development planning. The resulting

The following is an outline of the major components of PRISM. This model represents an adaption of Dr Madeline Hunter's Effective Teaching Model.

PRISM

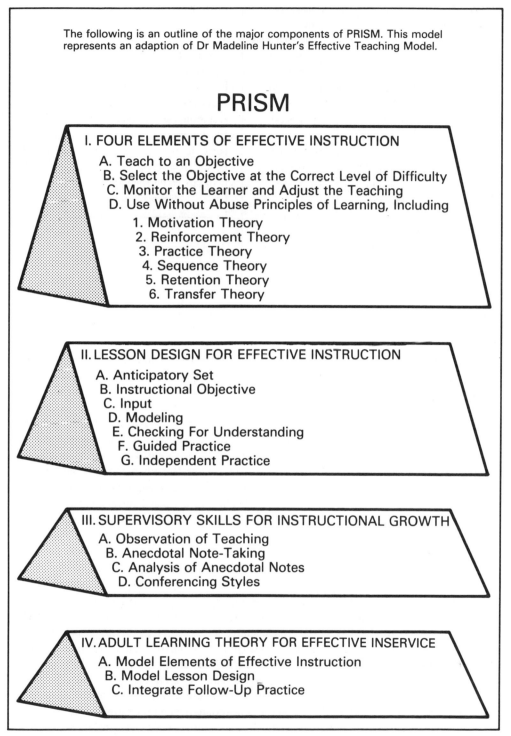

I. FOUR ELEMENTS OF EFFECTIVE INSTRUCTION
  A. Teach to an Objective
  B. Select the Objective at the Correct Level of Difficulty
  C. Monitor the Learner and Adjust the Teaching
  D. Use Without Abuse Principles of Learning, Including
    1. Motivation Theory
    2. Reinforcement Theory
    3. Practice Theory
    4. Sequence Theory
    5. Retention Theory
    6. Transfer Theory

II. LESSON DESIGN FOR EFFECTIVE INSTRUCTION
  A. Anticipatory Set
  B. Instructional Objective
  C. Input
  D. Modeling
  E. Checking For Understanding
  F. Guided Practice
  G. Independent Practice

III. SUPERVISORY SKILLS FOR INSTRUCTIONAL GROWTH
  A. Observation of Teaching
  B. Anecdotal Note-Taking
  C. Analysis of Anecdotal Notes
  D. Conferencing Styles

IV. ADULT LEARNING THEORY FOR EFFECTIVE INSERVICE
  A. Model Elements of Effective Instruction
  B. Model Lesson Design
  C. Integrate Follow-Up Practice

Figure 2.5   *The PRISM model*

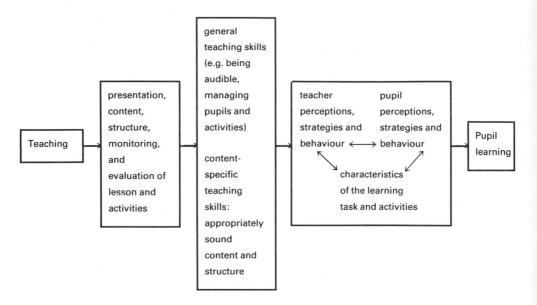

Figure 2.6 *A pedagogical (craft of teaching) level of analysis*
Source: Kyriacou (1986)

goals, which can be achieved both individually and collectively, can form a basis for teacher appraisal. There is, as we argue in the final chapter, a potentially very positive relationship between whole-school review, school development plans and teacher appraisal. Figure 2.7, taken from the GRIDS materials (Abbott *et al.*, 1988), summarizes one approach to selecting criteria as part of a whole-school review. Once such criteria have been formulated it is possible to discuss the balance between individual and collective action needed to achieve them.

Determining goals and striving towards them can be motivational, particularly when they are linked to feedback. Where goals are used in an appraisal scheme, they enable choices to be made from a vast range of criteria available from other sources, and consequently allow the appraisal to be targeted on areas for individual professional development. In these situations the goals themselves become criteria in the sense that their achievement provides the basis for the appraisal judgement.

While many criteria referred to in this section have been related to classroom performance it is important to bear in mind that, for some teachers, appraisal will also be concerned with management and pastoral tasks. Criteria for use in the appraisal of a teacher's management or pastoral role will therefore need to be drawn up. These could be derived from the appropriate literature, from experience and/or identified through goal setting in similar ways to this discussion on the criteria relating to teaching. The current emphasis on performance indicators (e.g. Hopkins and Leask, 1989) can also provide a source of criteria for appraisal. The list of potential indicators suggested by the Coopers and Lybrand report, *Local Management of Schools* provides a comprehensive list of such factors (see Figure 2.8).

A final point about criteria: in this discussion we have not made an explicit distinction between criteria and standards. Criteria in the sense we have used the term here refers to the specific focus of an appraisal activity; standards are to the quality of achievement in that activity or area. We must not be seduced into accepting mere coverage of a range of criteria as

In a review a set of criteria has two uses. The first is to set targets for development. The second is to judge the success of later development action. It is to be expected that criteria will emerge gradually during the period of review as different sources are tapped. However, there will come a time when two questions will need answers. The first is:

- Have we used the full range of appropriate criteria?

Answering this question will be easier if reference is made to Checklist 1 (below). The second question asks:

- For our review topic which *sources* of criteria have been explored?

Checklist 2 (below) is designed to elicit answers to this question.

The final step is to list against each of the selected criteria the evidence that has been used (to judge current practice) and will be used to judge the success of the later development changes.

Checklist 1 Range of criteria

With the focus of the review in mind, check the following and tick the column which applies. At the end of the review all areas should have a tick in the first column to show that each area has been considered. But perhaps criteria have been selected for only three areas. These three should be ticked in the second column. If it is inappropriate to have criteria in a particular area, then the final column should be ticked.

Criteria relating to	*Considered*	*Selected*	*Inappropriate*
Aims and intentions	. . .	. . .	. . .
Facilities and resources	. . .	. . .	. . .
Organisation and planning	. . .	. . .	. . .
Context of teaching	. . .	. . .	. . .
Processes of teaching	. . .	. . .	. . .
Attainment, achievement and outcomes	. . .	. . .	. . .

Checklist 2 Sources of criteria

For our review topic, which of the following sources of criteria have been explored? Tick the appropriate column.

Internal sources	*Yes*	*No*	*Not applicable*
Teacher opinion and experience	. . .	. . .	. . .
Documentary evidence (records)	. . .	. . .	. . .
Examples of pupils' work	. . .	. . .	. . .
Observations of practices	. . .	. . .	. . .
School documents	. . .	. . .	. . .
External sources			
Visiting	. . .	. . .	. . .
LEA documents	. . .	. . .	. . .
DES/HMI/research/documents	. . .	. . .	. . .
External consultant's views	. . .	. . .	. . .
Governors'/parents'/employers' views	. . .	. . .	. . .

Figure 2.7   *The final selection of criteria*

Source: Steadman *et al.* (1989). © SCDC Publications, 1989. Reproduced with permission

LIST OF FACTORS RELEVANT TO PERFORMANCE INDICATORS

Input Considerations:

(a) Pupil intake

Socioeconomic background

Cultural background

Innate ability

Handicaps

Levels of expectation by pupils and parents

Academic attainment on entry to each phase

(b) Resources

Number of teachers, by grade

Number of support staff, by type

Parental support (financial and otherwise)

Book and library provision

Technical facilities

Recurrent expenditure, by type

(c) Background

Accommodation levels and standards

Historical background

Stability of organization

School environment (neighbourhood)

Process Indicators:

(a) Staff

Teachers' characteristics, including qualifications

Staff demeanour

Staff sick leave

Teacher turnover

(b) Teacher deployment

Contact ratios

Class sizes

Mismatch (subject, experience, training)

(c) Curriculum arrangements

Core subject provision

Non-core subject options

Particularized provision

Examination options

Curriculum co-ordination

Curriculum documentation

(d) Wider educational practices

Provision of pastoral system

Structured sporting activities

Activities for the local community

Links with industry and commerce

Extra-curricular cultural activities

(e) Organization

Management delegation commitment

Pupil grouping provision

Homework policy and its applications

Involvement of governors

(f) Mutuality

Level of expectation of teachers

Level of responsibility given to pupils

Rewards/sanctions punishment systems

Outcome Indicators:

(a) Intermediate

Pupils' demeanour

Attendances, absenteeism, truancy

Lateness

Performance in internal activities

Participation in external activities

Indictable offences recorded

(b) Final for secondary schools

Performance in external examinations by age 16

Other intellectual attainments

Entry rates into continued and further education at age 16

Performance in external examinations from post-compulsory education

Participation in sporting, social, cultural activities post 16

Uptake of initial employment (relative to location)

Employment status at ages 21 and 25

The views of potential employers

(c) Final for primary schools

Academic attainments at age 11

Participation in sporting, social, cultural activities post 11

Figure 2.8 *Factors relevant to performance indicators*
Sources: Coopers and Lybrand (1988)

being the same as quality of performance. Criteria for standards also need to be worked out. Although this is probably best left to the appraiser and appraisee, those responsible for the management of the school need to be satisfied that the issues of both criteria and standards, of quantity and quality, are satisfactorily addressed.

Whatever decisions are made concerning criteria, they will be used at all stages of the appraisal process, including the data-gathering stages, some of which we now discuss.

DATA GATHERING

Data gathering is one of the most contentious and least understood components of the appraisal process. Within a professional development approach to appraisal, such as that adopted in this book, data gathering has two specific functions: the first is to provide information for the appraisal interview; the second is that data gathering is a professional development activity in itself. Consequently, it needs to be rigorously formative and supportive. Although classroom observation has an important role to play in data gathering, research evidence suggests that we should not view it as the sole source of data. However, as classroom observation has assumed such an important role in the appraisal process in England and Wales, we have decided to devote a separate chapter to it in this book.

Many argue for a variety of data sources to be used in teacher appraisal schemes (*vide* Millman, 1981). The contributors to the Millman handbook, for example, outline in practical detail eight sources of evidence for teacher appraisal: teacher interviews, teacher command of subject matter, peer review, classroom observation, student rating of instruction, student achievement as a measure of teacher competence, indirect measures, and staff self-evaluation. This is a similar list to others found in the literature: certainly Darling-Hammond and her colleagues (1983) discuss the same approaches, in a review which they conclude with this caveat:

> It is safe to say that research has not identified a teacher evaluation method which is unvaryingly 'successful'. This is not a surprising finding. A judgment of success depends on the purposes for which a technique is used as well as its ability to measure what it purports to measure. Some of these approaches seek to measure competence, while others that rely on direct observation seek to measure performance. Still others rely on student performance as a measure of teacher effectiveness, and by implication, teacher competence and performance. The generally low levels of reliability, generalizability, and validity attributed to teacher evaluation methods suggest that unidimensional approaches for assessing competence, performance, or effectiveness are unlikely to capture enough information about teaching attributes to completely satisfy any of the purposes for teacher evaluation.
>
> (Darling-Hammond *et al.*, 1983, p. 308)

It is obviously impossible in a review such as this to discuss in detail all the sources of data available for teacher appraisal. We therefore confine ourselves here to those which are either well known in the British context, have in our opinion an explicitly developmental focus, or provide a contrast to current practice.

Self-evaluation

Opportunities for self-assessment and reference to personal standards of performance strongly influence a teacher's sense of effectiveness and his or her motivation. It is also well substantiated that real and lasting change only occurs when an individual sees the need for it. Wise and his colleagues (1985) note that the teacher evaluation literature has recently begun to recognize the importance of self-assessment and of allowing teacher input into the determination of evaluation criteria and standards.

Approaches to self-evaluation obviously vary. There are the more quantitative approaches that encourage a teacher to use a set of performance criteria to analyse his or her teaching, and produce a descriptive profile of perceived practices. On the other hand there are the more open-ended approaches to self-review proposed by Stenhouse (1975) with his idea of the 'teacher researcher' and by Schon (1983) with his notion of the 'reflective practitioner'. These ideas, although potentially very powerful, espouse not so much the use of a specific technique but more a way of life.

Another approach to self-evaluation can be found in the use of adult learning contracts. Contracts provide a structure for learning and reflection which is specific, but allows for a great deal of teacher autonomy and exploration. Knowles' (1975; 1986) work on learning contracts is well known; less well known but perhaps more suited to our formative view of appraisal is the philosophy and methodology for self-directed learning proposed by Gibbons (Gibbons et al., 1980; Gibbons and Phillips, 1980) which has been put into a teacher education context by Hopkins and Norman (1982).

Peer Review

This approach has a great deal of potential not only for formative evaluation but also for developing a climate of professional development within a school. In this approach an individual or group of teachers evaluates a colleague's teaching. This process, as Darling-Hammond et al. (1983) noted:

> covers a broader spectrum of performance, encompassing not only performance in the classroom, but also intentionality (what the teacher intends to have happen) and other teaching behaviour as exhibited by assignment and grading practices. Although seldom used in formal teaching evaluations, the literature identifies many potential advantages to peer evaluation. The assumption underlying this approach is that peers are in the best position to assess competence, thus it suggests a professional conception of teaching work. Also, evaluators who are familiar with the classroom experience, subject matter, and demands on a teacher can render specific and practical suggestions for improvement.
>
> Peer evaluation in practice has received mixed reviews. Although a 3-year experiment including peer review was enthusiastically supported by the teaching staff in one district, another school district found that teachers lacked respect for evaluations by their peers and that the evaluations resulted in staff tension.

Student Evaluation

The use of students' opinions as a source of data for teacher appraisal is controversial. Teachers and heads tend to have reservations, but the evidence from both research and practice suggests that student data, when restricted to single descriptions of teaching practice, are quite valid. Student ratings of teachers' performance are of course another form of 'classroom observation' but this time from the students' perspective. Although usually applied at the college/university level many believe, as Darling-Hammond et al. (1983) demonstrate, that student ratings can be applied to secondary and primary school students. Commenting on this approach Darling-Hammond and her colleagues note that (1983, pp. 306–7):

The use of student ratings in evaluation assumes that: (a) the student knows when he has been motivated; (b) it is the student whose behaviour is to be changed; (c) student rating is feedback to the teacher, and (d) student recognition may motivate good teaching. This method is inexpensive with a high degree of reliability, usually ranging from 0.8 to 0.9 and above with some studies finding a modest degree of correlation between student ratings of teachers and student achievement.

Student Achievement

This is an even more controversial source of data. Most teachers and administrators claim that the ultimate purpose of appraisal is to improve a student's learning and education. Some interpret success in achieving this goal as being manifest in measured student achievement. Darling-Hammond and her colleagues are not entirely convinced by this argument. They say (1983, p. 307) that in

> an educational management system like teacher evaluation, student achievement must be measured in a manner consonant with the outcomes held to be important. Student achievement can be measured in many ways, comparing student test scores to a national norm; comparing test score gains with those of a comparable class; net gains over time, and so forth. Such scores, while representing legitimate and understandable indicators for many audiences, nonetheless require that numerous assumptions be made to link them to teacher competence or even teacher performance.
>
> Studies of the reliability of student test scores as a measure of teaching effectiveness consistently indicate that reliability is quite low, that is that the same teacher produces markedly different results in different situations, calling into question the use of such teacher effectiveness scores as an indicator of teacher competence. Further, the use of tests to measure teaching performance may inhibit curriculum innovation since teachers will tend to teach to the test, and may ignore or counteract the effects of teacher behaviours on other desirable outcomes.

With the form of the key stage assessment tests for the National Curriculum still somewhat unclear and given the difficulty of gauging the effects of context, we trust that this caveat, of the low reliability of test scores as a measure of teacher competence, is borne in mind if consideration is given to the use of these results as part of teacher appraisal.

All of these forms of data gathering together with the various approaches to climate setting and establishing criteria are described as 'ideal-types': they are approaches that have been found to work in various locations. By describing them in this way we do not wish to imply prescription, more to suggest them as an array of ideas that schools and LEAs may wish to employ or experiment with. In the following section we tread less speculative ground by discussing experiences with the preparation phase in the School Teacher Appraisal Pilot Study.

PREPARING FOR APPRAISAL: THE PILOT EXPERIENCE

In contrast to the 'ideal-types' described in previous sections of the chapter, the following account of the pilot experience of 'preparatory' appraisal activities, which is based on the evaluation report (Bradley et al., 1989), is neither as systematic nor comprehensive. It is from the comparison between the 'ideal' and the 'real', however, that others may gain their own sense of direction.

Climate Setting

Within the pilot study, perhaps the most important type of preparation has been the climate setting that has occurred as a result of the training that appraisers and appraisees have undergone. Training, as is seen in Chapter 7, has variously attempted to equip appraisers and appraisees to play different but complementary roles within the preparation and data-gathering phases. Although the onus of responsibility has tended to be on the appraiser, both roles are vital. As one appraisal co-ordinator remarked, 'If the appraisee skimps on preparation, they are doing themselves down. If the appraiser skimps, they are not doing justice to the appraisee.'

All pilot LEAs have provided supportive documentation for particular aspects of preparation and data gathering. Some schools have used the structure and documentation of their particular pilot scheme in a flexible manner, to suit their own circumstances. This seems to be the case particularly in schools that already had established procedures for staff development. Many appraisers and appraisees have derived great benefit and security from the documentation, finding it invaluable in this first stage of their understanding and practice of appraisal.

Across the pilots, there has also been a consistent and common emphasis on the value of the initial meeting as an element of preparation. In most authorities, a high value has also been placed on self-appraisal, in line with ACAS recommendation. In addition, we have seen varying importance given to the role of job descriptions, whole-school review, use of criteria, and other forms of data gathering both within and outside the classroom.

Initial Review Discussion

The importance of this meeting to the conduct of the rest of the process appeared crucial. Within the pilots, this was the occasion for establishing or confirming sound rapport between appraiser and appraisee, and clarifying, for both parties, what will happen and when. In the first round of appraisal in particular, it seems evident that the time committed to the initial discussion should not be skimped, if appraisees are to feel confident and clear about the process. Within the pilot there were wide variations in the time given to the initial meeting, ranging from five minutes to one hour. About half an hour seems to be the norm. Where care and time was taken, this usually led to the smooth running of the rest of the process.

Self-appraisal

For some teachers in the pilot study self-appraisal was the most significant part – 'the whole process wouldn't have been much without it'. Although teachers talked of the continuous self-appraisal that goes on in an informal way, many felt that the more systematic approach advocated in the pilot enhances the depth and quality of professional reflection. Some pilot authorities offered structured, supportive documentation for teacher self-appraisal. Such documents reflected the structure of the ACAS material, either in part or in whole, and many teachers have found this helpful.

There was evidence to suggest that teachers found it easier to be self-critical than to be positive about their strengths. One teacher's comment typifies this problem – 'I could have filled two pages with things I wasn't happy with but I found it difficult to write down what I felt I had achieved.'

There was also some uncertainty about how frank the teacher should be in reporting self-appraisal. For some, there was tension between being totally honest and screening out reflections which could possibly be misinterpreted or abused by the appraiser, or by others beyond the appraisal context – 'Are you trying to sell yourself or be honest?'

Some pilot LEAs believed that clear ground rules on confidentiality regarding self-appraisal needed to be established. Most of those involved in the pilot did not want complete sharing of self-appraisal, especially for less confident appraisees, even though such sharing did enrich communication and understanding in many appraisals. Two-stage documentation, which allows the appraisee to 'screen out' selected reflections for a second and public statement, was helpful in this respect.

There were variations in the sequencing of self-appraisal in the cycle. It was variously undertaken before the initial interview, after the initial interview and in parallel with classroom observation, or after classroom observation and as a result of a preparatory meeting for the interview. There was evidence that the appraisal interview and target setting were directly influenced by a teacher's self-appraisal. This particularly occurred where questions about future needs and directions were seriously addressed by the appraisee and discussed sympathetically with the appraiser. In these cases, well-structured self-appraisal informed the production of the agreed statements and the identification of targets.

Job Descriptions

In some cases, job descriptions were drawn up or clarified before the data-gathering stage. When available they provided a framework that has helped teachers work through their self-appraisal. Job descriptions were also used to identify a focus for classroom observation. Some pilot authorities regarded clarification and negotiation of job descriptions as an essential basis for appraisal; others did not. Producing job descriptions for teacher appraisal was a major task for many pilot schools and led, inevitably, to a greater need to identify whole-school issues and concerns.

These activities (training, the provision of documentation, initial meetings, self-appraisal, and job descriptions) constituted the main forms of preparation and climate setting in the pilot schemes. We found few examples of schools assessing themselves or being formally assessed for 'readiness' prior to involvement in appraisal. Despite this limited approach to preparation, particularly as compared with the 'ideal' types discussed earlier, there was evidence to suggest that the quality of shared understanding which evolved as a result of thorough preparation greatly enhanced the sense of purpose and effectiveness of the appraisal. But time required to prepare well continues to be a concern.

Whole-school Review

Some pilot authorities positively promoted the use of whole-school review as a contextual background against which individual teacher appraisal took place. Others maintained that the process could be equally beneficial if it started by diagnosing individual needs of staff, and used this information as a basis for formulating a 'whole-school' direction.

Where whole-school review did occur prior to appraisal, teachers were particularly aware of the purposes of appraisal. Many of those teachers welcomed having the whole-school framework as a reference point for identifying their own roles and responsibilities. This in turn led to greater clarity and better job satisfaction for many. Whole-school review can therefore play an effective preparatory and climate-setting role as well as providing a context for appraisal and school improvement.

Criteria in Appraisal

There was some uncertainty in most pilot LEAs' documentation and practice about the establishing of criteria and the making of judgements. Although the checklists or *aides-mémoire* of effective teaching techniques in pilot LEAs' documentation were often implicitly used as criteria, there was a general unease about the nature of the judgements made as a consequence of their application.

This tendency was also mirrored at the school level. The teachers we interviewed generally either claimed not to use criteria, or maintained that their criteria were intuitive. There was a general reaction against 'checklists', which most teachers regarded as criteria. There was little recognition that criteria could be established mutually, and that when they were, they could provide a significant aid to professional development. This lack of specificity in establishing a focus for appraisal was sometimes reflected in a vagueness in classroom observation and consequently could reduce the impact of appraisal.

Data Gathering

In this section of the chapter we briefly discuss the various approaches to data gathering (apart from classroom observation) employed in the appraisal pilot. Although the range of approaches was broad and imaginative, we must emphasize that, in general, classroom observation remained far and away the most common data-gathering activity.

Informed opinion   Although this practice was not widespread, there were a number of instances where preparation involved the collection of further informed opinion as a complement to self-appraisal and classroom observation. This involved the appraiser's approaching certain named individuals for their views about aspects of a teacher's work. Whilst the use of further informed opinion is a more generally recognized and integral part of headteacher appraisal, this is not yet the case for teacher appraisal.

Although it has the advantage of giving a broader and more informed perspective, the use of further informed opinion was generally seen as problematic. First, it involves more time; second, there is the danger of some colleagues being 'overused'; third, ethical 'ground rules' need to be established.

Pupil work and learning   The analysis of children's work and learning tended to arise naturally as a part of classroom observation, rather than as a separate data-gathering procedure. Information about children's work gathered from observation, and from discussions with children, was included in some of the feedback and interview sessions. We found no incidences of test scores or examination results being part of the appraisal process.

Work and curriculum plans   Some appraisers and appraisees examined weekly, termly or yearly plans in order to understand more fully the teachers' classroom context prior to observation. Daily record books were also discussed. Some of these discussions were especially helpful to the appraiser, as a means for extending their understanding of the appraisee's work, prior to observation and interview.

Information on responsibilities outside the classroom   For most appraisees the balance of information for the appraisal interview tended to focus on their classroom work. But there was scope in many of the self-appraisal pro formas for appraisees to reflect upon their role outside the classroom. There were wide variations in pilot LEAs in how extensively these reflections were used in the appraisal interview. The use of further informed opinion seems at present to be the most developed form of data gathering on managerial roles. Many appraisees felt daunted, initially, at the prospect of soliciting colleagues' views on their performance. In the event, this offered valuable insights which illuminated the appraisal interview. Some pilot authorities believed that 'the full role should be tackled' in data gathering, especially for middle and senior management. This was not done extensively in the pilot for appraisees other than headteachers.

SUMMARY OF KEY POINTS

In this chapter we have looked at various approaches to preparing for appraisal as they have suggested themselves from the literature, good practice and the experience of the School Teacher Appraisal Pilot Study. We have suggested that preparation for appraisal can fall into four categories: climate setting and readiness activities; whole-school review; establishing criteria; and data gathering. In reality we found that in the School Teacher Appraisal Pilot Study, preparation for appraisal occurred mainly during training and in the appraisal cycle itself, especially at the initial meeting. There were few examples of formal attempts at diagnosing the school's (or LEA's) organizational readiness for appraisal before proceeding. The exception was that whole-school review was successfully used as a preparatory activity in some LEAs. Whilst a number of data-gathering activities were used, none matched the importance given to classroom observation. Similarly, neither was the establishing of criteria for appraisal fully addressed.

Taking these findings as a whole and viewing them from the perspective of the British experience, we conclude that an appropriate ideal climate for appraisal will occur when the following conditions are met. Put another way, when an LEA or district or school is preparing for appraisal it should make certain that its planning and subsequent action is seen to:

- reflect a high level of commitment from the policy-making group (within the LEA or school), and reflect the educational values of the LEA, local area and school;

- encourage the assessment of a school's organizational readiness for appraisal and, if this is not high, encourage an open climate where staff are ready to collaborate and to discuss their work;

- emphasize the active involvement of teachers, particularly in establishing the rhythm of the process, and in planning for appraisal;

- place a high priority on training, especially for appraisers, that is designed to give teachers skills and confidence;

- place emphasis on both appraisers and appraisees having a clear understanding of the process and their responsibilities;

- be developmental and explicitly linked to staff development;

- consider the use of whole-school review as an implementation strategy for appraisal;

- encourage the collective establishment of criteria for appraisal that reflect a broad range of experience and are related to the educational aims of the school;

- utilize a methodology for appraisal that is valid, soundly based, that includes a variety of appraisers and data collection methods, but is *not* prescriptive;

- stress that classroom observation is one, but only one, way of collecting data for appraisal and encourage the widespread use of self-appraisal approaches.

Chapter 3

Classroom Observation

As we noted in Chapter 2, classroom observation is only one method of data gathering within appraisal, and needs to be seen in context, as a fertile but by no means comprehensive source of data on teacher performance. At the same time, classroom observation itself can be used to serve a variety of developmental purposes, some beyond the scope of an appraisal system. It would be wrong, therefore, to assume that data gathering within teacher appraisal and classroom observation are the same, and it is important to draw upon the full range of data sources referred to in Chapter 2.

Nevertheless, classroom observation does occupy a prominent position, both in the ACAS recommendations and in the School Teacher Appraisal Pilot Study. Yet the experience of these pilot schemes suggests that much of the potential of classroom observation is as yet unrealized, and many issues associated with carrying it out are still to be resolved. For these reasons a chapter has been devoted to this topic.

Even within appraisal the relative importance of classroom observation will vary from teacher to teacher. To quote the ACAS report, the importance of teacher observation will 'reflect the balance between the teaching load and other responsibilities outside the classroom' (ACAS, 1986, p. 5). This will vary over time as well as between teachers.

Classroom observation serves many purposes. It can be seen as an opportunity, following Joyce and Showers' (1980) model of teaching for coaching and feedback. It can also be used for monitoring, gathering data and evaluation. It can therefore be more or less developmental or evidential in purpose. It can be geared to individual development or be a vehicle for monitoring the achievement of school aims and objectives. It can be for the good of the observer or the observed, can promote self-reflection or mutual learning. It can monitor minimum competence or push for excellence. It can also serve one or several of these purposes at once. But there are choices to be made. Our aim in this chapter is to explore the scope of these choices. In the following section we discuss some of the main issues surrounding classroom observation. We then examine a number of different approaches to classroom observation before reflecting on the findings of the STAPS evaluation. We conclude by suggesting some guidelines for the implementation of the classroom observation phase of the appraisal process.

ISSUES IN CLASSROOM OBSERVATION

There is little in the way of a tradition of systematic classroom observation of teachers in the UK. While there are some signs that this position is changing, the norm is still one of classroom autonomy and relative isolation for teachers once they have successfully completed their probationary year. So it follows that the available literature on classroom observation relates to the use of classroom observation in a wider context than that of seeing how experienced teachers perform in class. In this section we discuss the debate between qualitative and quantitative approaches, the issues of criteria and making judgements, and the role of observation outside appraisal.

Qualitative v. Quantitative Approaches

At the heart of the classroom observation literature lies a concern with the concepts of validity and reliability and the avoidance of bias and subjectivity. These matters are at the centre of the debate between those who argue for quantitative as opposed to qualitative approaches to classroom observation. Quantitative approaches such as systematic classroom observation tend to utilize formal coding scales, which are then subjected to statistical analysis. Qualitative approaches such as ethnography and action research tend to use words to describe observed classroom interactions. There is obviously some common ground between the two groups. For example Croll, a systematic observer, argues that 'qualitative and quantitative techniques should not be regarded as mutually exclusive approaches but may be complementary' (1986, p. 8). Hammersley, an ethnographer, also seeks to play down controversy, arguing that we should 'renounce the temptation to treat systematic observation and ethnography as self-contained and mutually exclusive paradigms' (1986, p. 47). McIntyre and Macleod argue that 'flexible observation is best suited to generating useful perspectives and hypotheses and that systematic observation is best suited to provide precise descriptions and to test hypotheses' (in Hammersley *et al.*, 1986, p. 23). Nevertheless, the degree of predetermined structure in any observation instrument remains a useful point to consider. Whichever approach is chosen, 'descriptions of classrooms involve abstracting from the totality of the social world certain aspects thought to be relevant for particular investigatory purposes' (Croll, 1986, p. 4). In other words all observation is selective and there can be no one objective view.

Another way of looking at approaches to classroom observation is by an analysis of the types of instrument used. Evertson and Holley, for example, distinguish between (1) frequency/count systems, which take the form of category or sign systems; (2) rating systems; and (3) narrative systems of a more or less structured nature, ranging from attempts to write down quickly as much as possible to taking notes under specific set headings (in Millman, 1981). It is also possible to consider these techniques in terms of the 'technology' used. The various anthologies of observation instruments extend these ways of categorizing instruments. Simon and Boyer (1975) classify systems under:

- subject observation

- number of subjects observed

- collection methods reported

- category dimensions of the system

- settings in which used

- coding units

- collecting and coding personal needs

- uses reported by author

Galton adds further categories including reliability, consistency and training method and time (Galton, 1978). These categories are useful aids to thinking about any particular approach to observation.

Several further points can also be made about the choice of instrumentation. First, particular instruments tend to be suited to particular purposes of observation. Second, users need to decide whether to invent, adapt or adopt an instrument. Third, observers must realize that instruments inevitably have a point of view which may or may not be appropriate to the purpose of the observation or the reality of the particular classroom being observed.

Relevant here is another distinction that can be made in approaches towards classroom observation: the distinction between general and specific schedules. In the case of a general 'wide-lens' focus, the merits seem to be taking a look at a teacher whose work is not very familiar, or getting people used to observation. However, when it comes to fostering improvement, some kind of more specific approach seems to be required, for it is only by isolating and concentrating on areas for development that progress can be made.

Setting Criteria and Making Judgements

One approach is to go for 'value-free' observation, where the observer seeks simply to record factual information from the lesson. This is intended to provide the basis for factual feedback, designed to prompt the teacher to identify his/her own developmental needs. It is an approach well established in the action research tradition. Indeed action research is based on the idea of teachers deriving theory from a study of their practice and then using that theory to inform future practice. It depends on teachers receiving full and accurate factual feedback, preferably 'triangulated' from several sources so that data validity is enhanced. In this tradition, the observer's role is often referred to as 'critical friend'. It is an approach which is selective, focused and developmental. In reality this approach defers but does not remove the need for the establishment of criteria. The development of criteria tends to arise after feedback is given, at least in the first cycle of the observation and feedback spiral.

The alternatives involve bringing some degree of judgement into the observation at an earlier stage. The least satisfactory of these alternatives has the observer making unexplained and perhaps implicit judgements. Such judgements can seem close to prejudice and in any case cast the observer in the role of master to the observer as apprentice. Wragg (1987, p. 24) warns of the risks of projection and compensation. In the case of projection, the observer sees a lesson in terms of what s/he would do and in the case of compensation is excessively harsh, when s/he sees the teacher guilty of one of his/her own deficiencies. These are but examples to illustrate problems which can arise when judgements are made without reference to explicit and agreed criteria.

A better approach is to base schemes on predetermined, explicit criteria, so that the basis of judgement is out in the open for all to see. It is important that such criteria are understood by all concerned and shared, and that any judgements are made on that basis. Such criteria can of course be open to development in the light of experience. If the goal is commitment to change, then a discussion of criteria and agreement on which to use will need to occur between those who are observing and those who are being observed.

There appears to be a significant benefit in moving beyond facts towards interpretation based on agreed criteria. The key question seems to be about *when* criteria should be agreed. On balance we feel that determining criteria before observation makes sense where the observation is focused and planned. It enables greater purpose and direction. This does not, however, preclude the development of criteria in the light of the observation. The essential message appears to be that the teacher being observed needs to share in the interpretation process and avoid simply being told what the answers are. Day, in looking at classroom observation and appraisal, gives five principles for maximizing professional learning in this context:

a. learning requires opportunities for reflection and self-confrontation;

b. teachers and schools are motivated to learn by the identification of an issue or a problem which concerns them;

c. teachers learn best through active experiencing/participation;

d. decisions about change should arise from reflections upon and confrontations of past and present practice;

e. schools and teachers need support throughout processes of change.

(Day, 1987)

Such processes of professional learning depend on those engaged in observation and those being observed clarifying what counts as good practice in a particular context and deciding on what is evidence of the satisfactory accomplishment of that good practice.

The question that follows from this is where to get criteria from. It is possible, as we saw in Chapter 2, to derive criteria from a number of sources:

- effective teaching research

- principles of psychology

- experience

- individual, organizational or national goals

It is possible to use one or more of these approaches to formulate either before or after observation, a set of criteria, activities, behaviours, events or results, which if observed will indicate successful practice. It is perhaps useful to reiterate here the point also made in Chapter 2 about criteria and standards. It is not sufficient simply to set criteria; it is also necessary to assess quality in the meeting of these criteria. Such a setting of standards is probably best done between appraiser and appraisee, but an expectation of such qualitative judgements needs to be part of the appraisal scheme.

We should also add that the degree of judgement involved can also be related to the instrument used. There is a basic distinction between high- and low-inference instruments, which allow for more or less judgement on the part of the observer. There are also instruments which demand some type of rating of performance by the observer (e.g. HMI, 1982). We would, however, regard such technical issues connected with instrumentation as less significant than the need for any judgements to be based on explicit and explicable criteria.

Observation outside Appraisal

Observation does, can and should exist outside the framework of appraisal. It is an important approach to professional development which is not restricted to appraisers viewing appraisees. It may be sensible to regard the role of observation in appraisal as part of in-service activities that link to other aspects of the teacher's professional development. For example the observation phase of appraisal can also be used as an opportunity for peer coaching. In this perspective observation becomes one element of appraisal and can be used for a number of purposes. Its appropriateness in the context of appraisal will depend on the teachers involved and the goals set for a particular appraisal cycle.

DIFFERENT APPROACHES TO CLASSROOM OBSERVATION

Techniques for classroom observation vary tremendously, from the systematic approach advocated by Croll (1986) to the more formative and professional development approaches suggested by Acheson and Gall (1980) and Hook (1981). Here, we briefly discuss three different approaches to classroom discussion that have some potential for teacher appraisal and that we have described in detail elsewhere (Hopkins, 1985).

Clinical Supervision

This technique has enjoyed much popularity in North America, where it was developed as a method of supervising student teachers, but it is also suited for use in a wider range of classroom observation situations including teacher appraisal. It is a more structured form of peer observation which focuses on a teacher's instructional performance utilizing a three-phase approach to the observation of teaching events (*vide* Acheson and Gall, 1980; Goldhammer *et al.*, 1980; Cogan, 1973).

The three essential phases of the clinical supervision process are a planning conference, classroom observation and a feedback conference. The planning conference provides the observer and teacher with an opportunity to reflect on the proposed lesson, and this leads to a mutual decision to collect observational data on an aspect of the teacher's teaching. During the classroom observation phase, the observer observes the teacher teach and collects objective data on that aspect of teaching they agreed upon earlier. It is in the feedback conference that the observer and teacher share the information, decide on remedial action (if necessary) and often plan to collect further observational data. Variations on this process are suggested by different writers on the topic, but all follow the same basic pattern. It is important, however, to realize that to be effective all three phases of the process need to be gone through systematically (see Figure 3.1).

There are a number of principles that are important to consider in clinical supervision. First, the climate of interaction between teacher and observer needs to be non-threatening, helping and one of mutual trust. Second, the focus of the activity should be on improving instruction and the reinforcing of successful patterns, rather than on criticism of unsuccessful patterns, or changing the teacher's personality. Third, the process depends on the collection and use of objective observational data, not unsubstantiated value judgements. Fourth, teachers are encouraged to make inferences about their teaching from the data, and to use the data to construct hypotheses that can be tested out in the future. Fifth, each cycle of supervision is part of an ongoing process that builds on the other. Sixth, both observer and teacher are engaged in mutual interaction that can lead to improvement in teaching and observational skills for both.

Clinical supervision provides a model for classroom observation which can accommodate a variety of observation methods. We have already noted the distinction between qualitative and quantitative methods, and how they can apply within the clinical supervision cycle. Another way of regarding the qualitative and quantitative distinction is in the contrast between open and closed approaches. The former is about identifying hypotheses, the other about proving them. As Figure 3.2 illustrates, both approaches can be accommodated within the clinical supervision cycle.

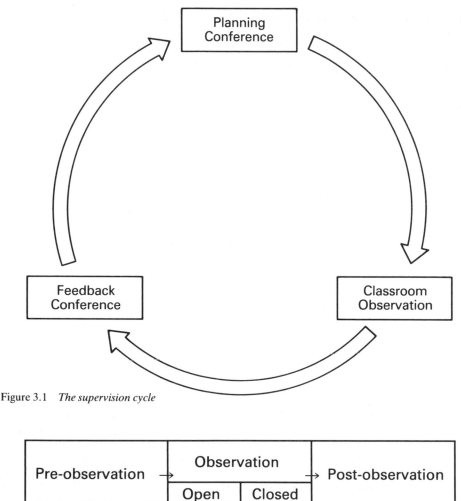

Figure 3.1 *The supervision cycle*

Pre-observation →	Observation		→ Post-observation
	Open	Closed	

Figure 3.2 *Open and closed observation within the clinical supervision cycle*

In the following discussion the semi-structured observation is of the open type, the coding scales of the closed variety.

Semi-structured Observation

This refers to simple observation schedules tailored by the teacher to fit a particular situation. When teachers observe each other teaching, all they often require are simple ways of gathering information on basic topics, such as questioning techniques, on-task and off-task behaviour and classroom management. It is usually preferable for teachers to devise their own observation schedules, to 'invent' them for a particular purpose. By doing this the teacher develops more ownership over the investigation and there is probably a better 'fit' between the object of the observation and the data-gathering method.

Before devising the observation schedule, it is useful to ask some organizing questions in order to ascertain the purpose of the observation. These questions are illustrative:

1 What is the purpose of the observation?

2 What teacher behaviours are worth observing?

3 What is focus of the observation?

4 What data-gathering methods will best serve the purpose?

5 How will the data be used?

Coding Scales

Although it may be preferable for teachers to devise their own observation scales, sometimes they may not have the time, or they may already be familiar with a rating or coding scale previously invented that fits their purpose.

The impetus for coding scales and checklists has come from North America where there is and has been a concern for 'scientific' approaches to teaching. This 'scientific' approach is seen in the emphasis on competency-based teaching, and behavioural objectives in curriculum planning and systematic instruction. It is unsurprising therefore to find that most coding scales available are American in origin. One of the problems with many American scales is that they are overly concerned with the formal teaching situation. Take for example one of the earliest and best known coding systems, the Flanders Interaction Analysis Categories (FIAC). This is widely used and has influenced the design of many other category systems. FIAC is based on ten analytic categories that reflects Flanders' view of teacher–pupil verbal interaction.

More recently, British researchers have been developing their own coding scales which, in general, stand in contrast to the American models. Galton (1978) comments:

> A feature of British research has been the wide variety of different organisational contexts within which classroom observation has been carried out. Much criticism has been directed at American systems because they often seem appropriate only to the more formal type of teaching situation. One of the most interesting features of the British research is the emphasis on observation in informal settings at one extreme and the variety of schedules suitable for use in the microteaching setting for the purpose of evaluating performance in questioning and lecturing skills at the other.

This quotation is taken from Galton's *British Mirrors*, a collection of 41 classroom observation systems that are British in origin. The majority of these instruments are junior and secondary school oriented but some are specifically designed for infant- or higher-education settings. Their target is almost exclusively teachers and pupils, most require only one observer and they are almost exclusively concerned with descriptions of classroom practice. The four major foci of these instruments are: classroom climate, organizational learning, the management and control of routine activities, and knowledge content. In general they are applicable across all curriculum areas.

In this section we have reviewed three approaches to classroom observation for teacher appraisal. Our argument is that some such approaches need to be formative and as far as possible constitute a professional development activity in themselves. We suggest that clinical supervision provides a basic format both for classroom observation and appraisal, and serves both these purposes. Clinical supervision is sufficiently flexible to accommodate both general and specific approaches, as well as internally developed observation schedules and externally developed coding scales. The choice of approach is of course related to the purpose of the observation as well as the professional judgement and needs of the teachers involved.

TWO EXAMPLES

In this section we provide two examples of how two of the STAPS schemes approached classroom observation and used some of the approaches described earlier.

Example 1

In the first case each pilot school developed its own appraisal scheme through a staff working group. This work was assisted by the project team, who produced guidelines and documentation. One of these booklets provided working groups with a range of questions to consider, including a series relevant to classroom observation. This aspect of appraisal was set firmly in a phase of 'preparation' for the interview and subsequently was referred to as 'looking at learning', 'action research into learning' and 'observation of teaching techniques'.

More detail was given in another document, where it was envisaged that teachers would work with colleagues in small support groups of two or more whose membership changed over time. These groups were 'formed initially from within an appraiser's team of appraisees'. The teachers carried out reciprocal observation, focused on issues and used criteria identified either in a pre-observation discussion or during a general look at a class. Observation was seen as the neutral collection of data and the post-observation conference for feedback and planning for development was mandatory. Information from this process went to the teacher's appraiser, if the appraiser did not carry out the observation in a particular year. Emphasis was placed on the importance in this 'classroom support exercise' of relationships, knowledge of context, techniques of observation, using observation as an aid for self-evaluation and practise in observation. As the scheme progressed the teachers involved used the classroom observation phase of appraisal to support the implementation of a variety of cross-curricular initiatives within their school. At the same time the project team was developing reporting forms and support documentation to assist the teachers involved. In these respects, therefore, this approach to appraisal was characterized by a concern with process questions. The aim was to harness individual commitment and develop a sense of ownership. In particular, classroom observation was seen as a collaborative venture in professional learning (Newcastle, 1987).

Example 2

The other LEA regarded appraisal as 'essentially school-based within the framework of the ACAS guidelines'. Four stages of the process were identified – teaching analysis and support (classroom observation), preparation for the appraisal interview, appraisal interview, and outcomes. There were two key features to plans for classroom observation. First, it was based on 'a statement of teaching policy with related prompt lists of criteria', developed by each school, with the aid of some guidance from the co-ordination team. Second, it was conceptualized within a framework of planning – analysis of teaching – feedback discussion, i.e. the clinical supervision cycle. By drawing attention to these two features, latitude was allowed in handling other issues as is shown in the following statement:

> The planning meeting will decide how the analysis will be conducted, what the support teacher will look for, how data will be gathered and recorded, how feedback will be provided and how often the teacher will be observed, and it will review carefully all relevant information. An important point is that the focus of the observation should relate to the agreed criteria.

The observer is referred to as the 'support teacher' who is seen as helping improve the performance of the observed teacher in a positive way. The role is that of critical friend, with the aim being to provide factual feedback on an agreed aspect of teaching in order to help the observed teacher work out his/her own development needs. Out of the process of observation and feedback comes a negotiated and agreed summary. This document summarizes what has been worked on and what results are to go to the appraiser, who is a separate person to the observer.

In addition to training teachers to adopt these principles, the LEA team provided a clear outline of procedures for observation, *Teaching Analysis and Support: Ten Steps* (Salford LEA, 1988b: see Figure 3.3) and a resource booklet, containing a range of observation techniques, from which observers can select.

These two examples illustrate one of the main themes of this chapter – the way in which the classroom observation phase can be used to support a range of professional development activities besides simply appraisal. In the following section we look more generally at the experience of classroom observation in the School Teacher Appraisal Pilot Study.

OBSERVATION IN PRACTICE: THE APPRAISAL PILOT EXPERIENCE

Classroom observation is an essential component of the appraisal process. This section draws on the experience of the six LEAs involved in the School Teacher Appraisal Pilot Study in integrating classroom observation into their appraisal schemes. The section is divided into three: the first briefly reviews the status of classroom observation as set out in the ACAS report; the second provides a synthesis of the views on and experience of classroom observation in the six LEAs involved in the pilot; the third raises a series of issues related to classroom observation based on the data collected during the evaluation.

ACAS and Classroom Observation

In the ACAS *Report of the Appraisal/Training Working Group*, classroom observation was seen as 'an essential feature of appraisal, but the purposes and objectives [were] to be fully investigated in the pilot project' (1986, p. 4). It seems fair to conclude that the view of the pilot study as a time for the 'design, testing and refinement of appraisal documentation', expressed in their report (ACAS, 1986, p. 7) applied especially to classroom observation. Consequently, classroom observation figured prominently in the plans of each of the six LEAs involved in the STAPS. Indeed at times classroom observation was seen by some teachers as being the whole of appraisal. This emphasis on classroom observation is also reflected in the NSG Report (1989).

Summary of Pilot LEA Positions

This is a brief and analytic synthesis of LEA positions based on our analysis of LEA documents and interviews with LEA co-ordinators set against the background of data collected as part of our evaluation work (Bradley *et al.*, 1989).

The *priority* given by LEAs to classroom observation was uniformly high. This priority however varied between LEAs. Some regarded classroom observation as simply one aspect of appraisal; others saw it as *the most important* aspect of the process.

The LEAs presented a uniform position on classroom observation *procedures*. All advocated a three-phase 'clinical supervision' cycle of preparation – observation – feedback, sometimes coupled with a tendency to move from general to more specific observations. All LEAs produced written materials of varying length and detail to provide guidance for appraisers and appraisees on classroom observation. These materials tended to focus on organizational and procedural matters rather than on the skills required for observation. Most

---

THE PLANNING MEETING

STEP 1   Does the teacher have a particular interest or concern they wish to follow up?

STEP 2   Help the teacher translate a particular focus into actions for you to observe

STEP 3   Arrange a suitable time to visit

STEP 4   Choose an analysis instrument appropriate to the focus

STEP 5   Find out about the lesson you are going to visit

STEP 6   VISIT THE CLASSROOM AND CARRY OUT THE AGREED ANALYSIS TECHNIQUE

THE FEEDBACK MEETING

STEP 7   Look at the information collected

STEP 8   Analyse the information

STEP 9   Interpret the information and draw out the teacher's reactions

STEP 10   Encourage the teacher to consider what was successful/unsuccessful.

Finally either plan for the next visit or agree and record one or two objectives

---

Figure 3.3   *Procedures for observation: checklist*
Source: Salford LEA (1988b)

LEAs advocated a 'variety of approaches' for classroom observation (checklists, coding scales or open-ended approaches). Most observations were carried out by the same person who conducted the appraisal interview.

Each LEA required that *feedback* following observation be given within 48 hours. In most cases some form of immediate feedback was given which was followed by a more extended discussion within 48 hours and the production of a written statement.

The *link* between classroom observation and the appraisal interview was established by some form of written record. The quality of this record was of course mainly contingent on the quality of the observation itself, and was related to the skill level of the observer and the materials that supported the observation. There was a wide variety in all these variables both within and between LEAs.

Some Practical Issues

1 'Dry runs' of classroom observation were sometimes seen as effective in reducing initial anxieties and in providing a clear view of what the process involved. This initial apprehension also tended to disappear in the light of experience with observation.

2 The idea of balancing general and specific observation approaches appeared to gain ground during the pilot, with general observation often being recommended for a first observation as a means of identifying areas for specific focus during subsequent observations. Some teachers found choosing areas for specific focus quite difficult, and needed to carry out an initial general observation in order to identify such areas.

3 We found a wide variation over how openly and fully notes were taken by the observer during lessons. We often found observers relying on notes structured by predetermined headings, or simple schedules. Some of the observation records we saw suggest that some observers are not yet very skilled in producing objective data that can be used for developmental purposes. In these cases records were typically a series of judgements, not a factual basis for formative discussion.

4 When an LEA provided resource books of observation instruments, teachers tended to choose from this particular variety of approaches. Besides providing such a resource book, one LEA provided a 'step by step' guide to carrying out observation, as mentioned earlier. The availability of this kind of support enhanced the quality of classroom observation.

5 There was also variety in the scheduling of observation. In some cases there was a series of three or more observations over a period of less than three weeks and sometimes within one week. In other situations a series of observations was spread over a much longer period. A third approach was to restrict observation to 15–25 minutes, using that time to focus on a specific aspect of classroom life. The NSG Report (1989) suggests that the appraisal process occurs within a period of half a term. This conflicts somewhat with our findings that a spread of observations on an agreed focus over a longer period of time provides more scope for a teacher's professional development.

6 There was, however, some difficulty in ensuring that development occurred following classroom observation. There was sometimes a gap between the quality of experience reported to us by observers and the quality of feedback recounted to us by the observed. Where preparation and training for observation and feedback was done well, changes in teaching practice often occurred.

7 Many teachers found observation useful in itself. In these cases the major outcome was that it encouraged appraisees *and* appraisers to reflect more systematically on their teaching and most found this was a most rewarding professional experience. But these professional

development aspects of classroom observation were not exploited systematically during the pilot.

8   Despite the commitment to appraisal for professional development within the pilot study, LEAs varied on how far they regarded classroom observation as developmental. A number of factors appeared to limit its developmental impact. The distinction between general and specific observation was seen by some as a means of combining accountability purposes via the general observations with developmental purposes via the specific observations. Besides this confusion of purpose, other problems in the pilot study were the limited time given to observation, and the frequent use of non-specialist appraisers. The lack of specific observation skills limited the ability of an observer to work alongside the teacher as a coach. Finally, although there was reference in LEA documentation to linking teacher appraisal to whole-school review or curriculum implementation, the links were not explicit or obvious in the day-to-day reality of the appraisal process.

SUMMARY AND KEY POINTS

There is no evidence for one best way of carrying out classroom observation. In addition, the variety of choice of methods is even greater in classroom observation than for other parts of the appraisal process. As we have seen, there are many alternatives for selecting the best approach for a particular purpose. We have also noted the pitfalls. The main dangers appear to be subjectivity, arbitrary judgements, bias, use of poorly understood instruments and failure to provide feedback or prepare for the observation. Once again, there is a case for a flexible, rational, open and objective approach, supported by training and resulting in follow-up action.

In our opinion, classroom observation is a very complex activity. In terms of appraisal for professional development its success depends on the following factors.

Development of Observation Skills

This discussion has highlighted the need for specific skills training for classroom observation. These skills concern the ability to handle the clinical supervision process, to be 'objective', to establish trust and confidence, and to negotiate criteria. They need to be developed over time, through ongoing training, practice and feedback.

Clinical Supervision

The seeming complexities of classroom observation can be resolved by using the clinical supervision model. The three-stage approach accommodates both elaborate procedures and simple instruments because their use is decided on by the teachers involved.

Appropriate Procedures and Approaches

Both general and specific approaches to observation can be used, but specific approaches appear to have most potential for enabling development. What most teachers require, however, is the acceptance of the need for flexibility of approach, in terms of focus and instruments, according to school and individual needs. Teachers, when they move away from notes, appear quite capable of adapting instruments and simplifying them to suit their own purposes. The logical consequence is for LEA appraisal co-ordinators to make handbooks of instruments available for reference.

Use of Criteria in Observation

Criteria for observation can be negotiated during a pre-observation meeting, or relate to an analysis of a teacher's job, the setting of targets, or to the school's teaching policy statement. Our own view is that all of these approaches are acceptable as long as the question of criteria is not fudged. If it is, then the whole appraisal process is in danger of degenerating into a paper exercise.

Objective Records and Formative Dialogue

Our view is that in appraisal for professional development the person doing the classroom observation need not be the appraised teacher's head or work group leader. We see great opportunities for professional growth in peer observation, but in these situations two considerations need to be borne in mind. The first is that an adequate record should be made of the observation that can be fed into the appraisal interview and the other is that an effective formative dialogue should occur as a result of the observation.

Observation outside Appraisal

Given the limited time available for observation within appraisal and the value teachers appear to place on it as a collaborative learning exercise, there seems to be a case for developing more observation outside the confines of appraisal.

Chapter 4

The Appraisal Interview

The appraisal interview is at the hub of the appraisal process. The information gathering and preparation activities before it can, as indicated, serve as opportunities for development in themselves. The degree of such development provides one measure of their success. Nevertheless, within the appraisal process, the information gathering and preparation activities can only be considered truly successful if they enable a productive appraisal interview to occur. Such an interview should provide an opportunity for reflection on previous work with the aim of agreeing plans for the future. It is potentially a sensitive occasion, dealing as it does with matters at the heart of a teacher's career and job. It is also an occasion that can trigger further development and growth.

In this chapter we survey lessons from the appraisal and general management literature relevant to the interview and also consider experience from the School Teacher Appraisal Pilot Study. We then draw together some key points of advice.

To provide a context for the rest of the chapter, we begin by clarifying the scope of a typical appraisal interview. Essentially it includes the following elements:

- a *review* of work done and targets achieved since the previous appraisal;

- setting *targets* for the future both for developing the present job and for professional and career development;

- identifying *ways* of achieving these targets and criteria for their successful accomplishment;

- agreeing a final *record* or statement of the appraisal.

As an opportunity to review past performance and agree future plans, it serves as a focal point in the wider appraisal process.

ISSUES IN APPRAISAL INTERVIEWING

A review of appraisal and management literature reveals that criticisms of appraisal practices tend to apply with most force to the interview stage. For example, Stenning and Stenning (1984, pp. 79–80) identify three common failings in appraisal schemes. First, they argue that such schemes often fail to secure the commitment of some or all of the participants 'largely because appraisers lack adequate training and convey that they begrudge the time it takes to carry out the procedures'. Second, Stenning and Stenning, drawing on social psychology, refer to a number of threats to objectivity such as 'the "halo effect"; "primacy and recency"; "constant error"; "stereotyping"; "projection"; "implicit personality theory"; "central tendency"' etc. Third, they criticize schemes which degenerate into 'going through the motions': because 'little attempt may be made to incorporate assessments into any corporate or individual planning framework'. They and others touch on the potential difficulties for working relationships posed by the appraisal interviews. The danger highlighted is that both appraiser and appraisee can avoid issues in the interests of avoiding unpleasantness or creating ill feeling. Meyer, looking at experiences with appraisal at the General Electric Company in the 1960s, makes these points:

- Criticism has a negative effect on achievement of goals;

- Praise has little effect one way or the other;

- Performance improved most when specific goals are established;

- Defensiveness resulting from critical appraisal produces inferior performance;

- Coaching should be a day-to-day, not a once-a-year activity;

- Mutual goal setting, not criticism, improves performance;

- Interviews designed primarily to improve a man's/woman's performance should not at the same time weigh his/her salary or promotion in the balance;

- Participation by the employee in the goal-setting procedure helps produce favourable results.

(Meyer *et al.*, 1965)

In developing these contentions, Meyer questions the value of appraisal systems that rested on an annual interview, arguing the need for 'day-to-day' dialogue. He argues that 'employees seem to accept suggestions for improved performance if they are given in a less concentrated form than is the case in comprehensive annual appraisal; where criticisms could mount, leading to an "overload phenomenon"'. He also argues that 'studies of the learning process point out that feedback is less effective if much time is allowed to elapse between the performances and the feedback' (Meyer *et al.*, 1965, p. 127).

The force of these criticisms is not to destroy the case for appraisal interviews but first to present a series of problems, which have to be tackled to ensure the success and credibility of the interviews and secondly to point to the need for a discussion about the frequency of interviews and their relationship with the rest of the appraisal process. These criticisms draw attention to the need to see the interview as one aspect of regular and ongoing discussion. Gill (1977), in a review of appraisal in UK companies conducted in the 1970s, points to some solutions to potential problems, arguing that 'training is essential for effective appraisal interviewing'. Then, drawing from a review of the literature on appraisal interviewing, Gill suggests that the following are linked to success in such interviews:

1 A high level of subordinate participation in the appraisal process.

2 A helpful and constructive attitude (as opposed to a critical one) on the part of the appraiser.

3 A problem-solving approach by the interviewer (as opposed to a 'tell and sell' style).

4 Participation by the employee in setting any specific goals to be achieved.

Gill goes on to stress, with reference to Fletcher's study of the Civil Service, that a problem-solving approach to interviews, 'with or without discussion of weaknesses, elicited a favourable attitude to appraisal in a greater number of cases than did the "tell and sell" approach'. This advice is set in the context that 'the formal interview should be seen, however, as merely one event in a continuing relationship of informal communication between superior and subordinate'. Such an approach would seem to provide an antidote to Meyer's concern.

Reflecting a different background – an approach that uses learning theory as the basis for professional development with North American teachers – Hunter offers the following advice on 'evaluative conferences' – i.e. appraisal interviews:

> An evaluative conference should be the summation of what has occurred in and resulted from a series of instructional conferences. Information given and conclusions reached in an evaluative conference should come as no surprise to the teacher because the supporting evidence has been discussed in previous instructional conferences. As a result, the evaluative conference has high probability for being perceived as fair, just and supportable by objective evidence rather than based on subjective opinion. This conference is the culmination of a year's diagnostic, prescriptive, collaborative work with a teacher and supervisor who shared responsibility for the teacher's continuous professional growth.
>
> This growth will occur more rapidly and predictably if the teacher's effort and growth is rewarded, and any professional gaps or deficiencies are interpreted in perspective rather than being over-emphasised because a teacher doesn't immediately become the perfect model of the ideal educator. When administrators and supervisors work with teachers, as teachers are expected to work with students, supervision will become a more highly skilled and respected function in our profession.
>
> (Hunter, 1980, p. 412)

While this advice reflects Hunter's particular technique and use of highly trained supervisors, it does contain points of general interest. The context of the interview is clearly important but once the interview begins the tone and atmosphere are crucial.

In particular, attention is drawn to the need to consider how teachers learn. Positive reinforcement, building on strengths, ongoing support and encouragement, typical features in teaching generally, need to be applied to teachers by each other.

The following suggestions from *Those Having Torches* draw together the advice we have so far surveyed:

> The appraiser should create a climate in which genuine dialogue can take place. The conditions for the interview should be comfortable, quiet and uninterrupted. Adequate time should be allocated for the interview and it should begin with the teacher's view of his/her performance during the past year. Attention should be focussed upon past successes and the data available should also be used to help indicate areas for improvement including ways by which this might be achieved. The teacher's interests and aspirations should be given attention, and the discussion should then move into a consideration of suitable targets for the following year. Above all, the focus should be on performance in the defined job rather than on personality.
>
> (Suffolk Education Dept, 1985, p. 6)

What comes across is the need to set the main appraisal interview alongside more frequent, ongoing feedback and dialogue. Adair (1983, p. 123) for example, stresses that 'you should see the formal system as at best a safety net for a process that should be going on continually'. Drawing upon the work of Lawrence Russell of the Engineering Training Board, he offers guidelines for appraisers and appraisees. Taken as a whole they reflect a concern for the appraisal interview to be supportive and structured. Attention is drawn to the need to take steps to reduce tension and to conduct the interview in a calm and frank manner. What also comes across is a case for appraisers to listen carefully to appraisees and to involve them fully in discussing future plans. Finally, advice is given on the need to avoid unsubstantiated discussion, destructive criticism and unrealistic plans. A picture is thus beginning to emerge of consistent advice among the various writers about appraisal interviewing.

Adair also draws attention to some of the communication skills essential for successful interviews. Basically these skills include such things as questioning, listening, clarifying and summarizing skills. They also include an ability to react to and interpret non-verbal communication – 'body language'. Developing a repertoire of such skills necessitates training. Allinson (1977) for one, carried out a study of the effects of a training course for managers in appraisal interviewing and found that a 'role-playing approach to performance appraisal interview training was successful at all managerial levels in a large organisation'. He offered the caution that 'mid-career managers may have the most to gain from training'. Such skills need to be developed and then carried out in the context of a problem-solving approach. Such skills do, of course, have far wider application than just in appraisal interviews and are in fact part and parcel of effective management.

The literature thus offers some advice and guidelines for the conduct of appraisal interviews. A further point of importance concerns how the appraisal is summarized or recorded. Armstrong (1977) identifies the following techniques:

- overall assessment

- guideline assessment

- grading

- merit rating

- critical incident method

- results-orientated schemes

He argues for the advantages of properly conducted results-orientated schemes, where the aim is to relate appraisal to jointly agreed targets and goals. He feels this approach offers three advantages:

1 The subordinate is given the opportunity to make his own evaluation of the results he obtains. When he is discussing results and the actions that produced those results, he is actually appraising himself and gaining insight on how he can improve his own methods and behaviour.

2 The job of the manager shifts from that of criticising the subordinate to that of helping him to improve his own performance.

3 It is consistent with the belief that people work better when they have definite goals which they must meet in specified periods.

(Armstrong, 1977, p. 169)

We return to the question of target setting in the next chapter, which is concerned with ensuring that something happens as a result of appraisal. At this juncture we wish to draw attention to the point that the appraisal interview should result in clear and agreed action plans and targets for the future. There is also a need for a written record of such targets and of the main points of the interview discussion, to provide a source of reference for future review meetings or interviews. In essence it is an acceptance by appraiser and appraisee of what has been agreed between them and serves as an *aide-mémoire* to support appropriate future developments. It is a guarantee that promises, commitments and plans will not be forgotten.

EXPERIENCE FROM THE SCHOOL TEACHER APPRAISAL PILOT STUDY

The lessons from the literature, reflecting as they do experience with appraisal interviewing in a range of situations, are fairly consistent. We now compare these with the experience gained from the School Teacher Appraisal Pilot Study.

The lessons provided by the pilot LEAs concerning the appraisal interview reflect the type of advice given in the literature. They can be considered in terms of how they relate to the preparation, structure, style and results of appraisal interviews.

Preparation

The need for preparation by both appraiser and appraisee was stressed in LEA guidance and found important in practice. Preparation worked best if it involved the consideration of job descriptions and of data gathered during the appraisal process. For appraisees self-appraisal provided an important means of getting ready for the interview. However, studying data and self-appraisal by themselves provided only preparation of a general sort. The need was for some process to be built in to enable this general preparation to be channelled towards the interview. In other words, an agenda-setting process was necessary, a process sometimes facilitated by the use of an interview preparation form (a form available in advance, on which appraiser and appraisee add comments relating to agenda items). This form could then be reflected on before the interview and could serve as the basis of discussion. Alternatively, a pre-interview meeting (used to review data gathering and set an agenda) could be used. Preparation for the interview also appeared a 'nuts and bolts' business of fixing a suitable time, booking a suitable room and ensuring adequate time would be available.

Structure

We noted a variety of approaches in the pilot study to setting the interview agenda. Among the options used were structuring the interview around self-appraisal forms, interview preparation forms, job descriptions or classroom observation notes.

The nature of the agenda also related to the issue of how general the interview was. Sometimes, particularly in headteacher appraisal, the preference was to select perhaps three key areas of responsibility to focus on. There was also some evidence to suggest that if teachers are appraised 'generally' in the first appraisal cycle, it may be useful and desirable for them to be appraised on specific aspects of their performance subsequently. Such selected areas of focus might be determined either at the initial meeting or as a result of what emerges from data gathering. Where this happens the selected areas of focus would form the basis of the interview agenda. Sometimes some combination of the approaches we have noted provided the agenda. We did not find one best all-purpose structure although Figure 4.1 illustrates the range of areas typically addressed. What was important was the need for both parties to be clear beforehand about the agenda, so that they could come prepared. It was seen as important for there to be 'no surprises' at the interview in terms of items raised.

We have drawn attention in this section to the value of a clear agenda, agreed beforehand, in promoting an effective interview. Our feeling is that the exact nature of the agenda is

1 A review of the appraisee's job description.

2 A review of the appraisee's general work and work on targets since the last interview:

- successes

- difficulties and areas for development

- constraints

3 Discussion of future plans:

- job-related plans

- other professional development plans

- career-related plans

4 Setting targets and agreeing ways of achieving targets and criteria, dates for their accomplishment, necessary action and support.

5 Conclusion.

(Item 5 can be used to clarify responsibility for writing up the appraisal statement. The appraiser would normally take notes during the interview and write these up afterwards. The written-up version is then checked and agreed by the appraisee.)

Figure 4.1 *A typical interview agenda*

less important. What matters is that there is one, and that it is followed. While agreeing an agenda beforehand appeared to share the responsibility for keeping to it between appraiser and appraisee, our experience in the pilot study also convinced us of the key role of the appraiser in managing the pace and flow of the interview. Without such management, even a clear agenda could prove inadequate. Also needed were skills in focusing the discussion, opening up and closing down topics, and in moving from a general airing of views to formulating specific targets.

Style
Careful preparation in the early parts of the appraisal process appeared helpful in ensuring a successful interview in the pilot study. To facilitate this, the pilot LEAs gave a good deal of advice on the style and tone of the interview. Such advice on style typically included the following points:

1   The interview should take place in comfortable surroundings and be free from interruptions and distractions.

2   There should be adequate time available and no pressing deadlines.

3   It should be a joint discussion in which the appraisee should have full opportunity to talk freely, perhaps talking for 80 per cent of the time at the start of the interview and for 50 per cent of the time in the final stages.

4   A problem-solving approach is desirable.

5   There should be no surprises in terms of items raised.

6   The focus should be on performance, not personality and on matters capable of development.

7   The overall tone should be 'comfortable but not cosy', positive, constructive, frank, realistic and supportive.

Indeed some LEAs preferred to change the term 'interview' to 'conference' or 'dialogue' to help emphasize these points by drawing attention to the two-way nature of the process.

An analysis of the advice on style shows much of it to be practical and amenable to planning. Other advice depends on training, and we noted in the pilot study that extra care was needed when appraisers and appraisees had received different amounts of initial appraisal training. Interviews appeared to be facilitated when both appraisers and appraisees had had training relating to the interview and had had an opportunity to participate in 'mock' interview exercises. Such exercises provide a chance to practise the listening, questioning, summarizing and clarifying skills referred to earlier. The typical 'triads' interview exercise used in training provided a good basis for the development of these and other interview skills. In it teachers form groups of three and hold practice interviews, with each teacher taking on in turn the roles of appraisee, appraiser and observer. The feedback role of the observer is particularly import-ant in sensitizing people to questions of interview style and technique. However, as with other aspects of the appraisal process, subsequent practice in 'real' interviews appeared best (in terms of allowing the development of skills), if it followed quickly on initial training.

The teachers and headteachers in the School Teacher Appraisal Pilot Study tended to regard the appraisal interview as the most significant part of the process and also found it beneficial in a number of typical ways. It was seen as a chance to discuss a range of issues in depth, share ideas, air views and clear the air. It provided the forum for reassurance, praise, recognition and support. The following comments illustrate some of these points:

'it's quite exhausting, talking in a way that you don't normally do but also refreshing';

'it made me think more logically and clearly about the targets set and helped me to plan. Nice to look back and to see what had got done. Nice to have the time with the headteacher individually, thinking about yourself, your development';

'it has made me a much more self-aware teacher; it helped me to discover what I am doing and why, and to understand why I like teaching';

'a useful opportunity to clarify and articulate ideas';

'a lovely opportunity to sit back and look at what you've done . . . time to think about things';

'it's helped me draw the needs of my class to the senior management';

'it helps you focus on what you should be doing'.

The Cambridge Institute Evaluation Report identified a list of factors conducive to successful interviews similar to those outlined in this chapter (Bradley *et al.*, 1989). The report also identified factors that appeared to undermine successful interviews:

- inadequate time;
- low priority;
- sudden changes in the planned programme;
- lack of preparation by either or both parties (our evidence suggests that this is usually, but not always, on the part of the appraisee);
- not keeping to the agenda;
- interruptions.

SUMMARY OF KEY POINTS
To avoid these difficulties we would draw attention to the following points of advice:

Planning
Appraisal interviews appear to be most effective if an agenda is agreed in advance. An agenda-setting meeting a few days before the interview helps to focus attention on what is to happen and serves as a spur to reflection and preparation by both appraiser and appraisee prior to the interview. It helps to ensure both come to the interview familiar with materials and data to be considered. An agenda also helps to make the interview feel purposeful, systematic and productive.

Purpose
Clarity on the purposes of an appraisal interview is needed. Such clarity is partly achieved through setting an appropriate agenda. However, it needs to be remembered that the interview is concerned with the review of professional performance and planning for the future. Its scope is determined by the focus of the appraisal and the teacher's job description, so certain topics will therefore be inappropriate for discussion in this forum. Further, the line between appraisal and counselling needs to be drawn. An appraiser may feel as a result of what the appraisee says that further counselling is needed, but will need to consider the need for follow-up discussions to deal with areas not strictly within the province of an appraisal interview.

We would recommend that the appraiser reminds the appraisee of the purposes of the interview at an early stage and ends the interview by reviewing with the appraisee whether it has achieved its purposes.

Managing the Interview
Clarifying purposes at the start of the interview and keeping to an agreed agenda ought to help give the interview a sense of direction. Beyond this, while we believe both parties have a responsibility to make the interview work, we would draw attention to the need for the appraiser to use communication skills to best effect. In particular the appraiser needs to use different styles of questioning – open questions, for example, to encourage the appraisee to

explore topics and direct questions to focus the discussion or draw an area of discussion to a close. Similarly, at the end of each agenda item, the appraiser needs to summarize what has been agreed and check that both people have the same understanding of this. Further, in the final stages of the interview, the appraiser needs to review agreed targets and clarify for the appraisee what will happen as a consequence of the interview. In other words, the aim is to be logical and systematic.

Attention to Environment

For the advice given so far to work both appraiser and appraisee need to feel at ease. A comfortable, quiet interview location, free from interruptions is the ideal.

Developing Appropriate Interpersonal Skills

Above all the interview needs to be a time for genuine dialogue conducted in a supportive atmosphere. The aim is to achieve a sense of being on the same side. Careful listening to what is said will help here as will a determination to enable the appraisee to have his or her full say. Care also needs to be taken to be receptive to non-verbal communication.

Outcomes

A number of important benefits can occur during the appraisal interview. It provides an opportunity for praise, recognition, 'clearing the air' and resolving problems. However, the interview is also the trigger for future development. It is here that care over target setting and planning for the future is needed. It is to this topic that we turn in the next chapter.

Chapter 5

Appraisal, Development and Target Setting

Throughout this book we have argued that appraisal is a valuable means of promoting the professional development of teachers and their schools. We have taken the view that development can occur in each phase of the process, that is during the preparatory, interview and follow-up stages. Such development appears to arise in part from the way appraisal can, at various points, prompt reflection and increase self-awareness. It also appears to arise from the potential of the process for clarifying aims and priorities and for bringing about a clearer definition of responsibilities. Furthermore, development appears possible as a result of the opportunities provided by appraisal for collaborative work and better communication.

While much development is possible in the earlier stages of the process, something is lost if adequate care is not taken over the follow-up stages. The literature on both appraisal and experience from the School Teacher Appraisal Pilot Study emphasizes the importance of what happens as a result of the appraisal interview. Turner and Clift (1988, p. 191) for example identified potential problems in this area as a result of their research:

> One of the main concerns teachers have about appraisal is that it will prove costly in terms of time but will have little impact in terms of bringing about improvements ... we have drawn on data from the case studies to show the concern of many teachers that if there is to be an appraisal of a member of staff there must be some kind of follow-up and that this can be in the form of 'target setting'. Despite such concerns it is evident that in many cases appraisals were not followed up and produced little or nothing that was tangible. The lack of any decisive change produced scepticism on the part of many teachers as to the real value of having an appraisal scheme.

Clearly if such scepticism arises it presents a real threat to the success of appraisal as an ongoing and regular process.

In part, therefore, the success of appraisal in developmental terms relates to the management of the interview and the way the resulting agreed statement/action plans are formulated. Success at the follow-up stage also depends on how that stage is itself managed.

In this chapter we draw some lessons from the literature on strategies for ensuring that appraisal leads to professional development. We then compare these lessons with pilot study experience in order to derive some practical guidance.

ENSURING DEVELOPMENT OCCURS DURING THE APPRAISAL PROCESS

An effective way of linking teacher development to appraisal during the process itself is through the use of data gathering and other appraisal methods that have a developmental focus. Each stage of the process can, as we have attempted to show, be carried out in such a way as to emphasize its developmental potential. For example, in the case of classroom observation, a 'clinical supervision' format can be used to ensure that the teacher is given feedback on specific areas in such a way as to encourage development and change. Stenhouse's and Schon's notions of the 'teacher researcher' and 'reflective practitioner' can be used to inform thinking about self-appraisal, and the type of thinking they embody serves as justification for giving prominence to its use. Indeed the presence of self-appraisal provides an important means of generating teachers' commitment to the appraisal process.

There are also many opportunities arising from appraisal for teachers to collaborate and work together in a supportive and critical community. These occur at a variety of points during the process. Many of them have been described in a book by Loucks-Horsley and her colleagues (1987). Their list of collaborative approaches for staff development contains strategies we have already identified as potential components of an appraisal process. The more these can be integrated into an appraisal scheme, the more participating in appraisal can become a major professional development activity. The critical attributes of successful staff development programmes as identified by Loucks-Horsley *et al.* (1987, p. 8) display a startling compatibility with many of the themes discussed in this book:

Collegiality and collaboration

Experimentation and risk taking

Incorporation of available knowledge bases

Appropriate participant involvement in goal setting, implementation, evaluation, and decision making

Time to work on staff development and assimilate new learning

Leadership and sustained administrative support

Appropriate incentives and rewards

Designs built on principles of adult learning and the change process

Integration of individual goals with school and district goals

Formal placement of the program within the philosophy and organizational structure of the school and district.

In other words those responsible for appraisal schemes will need to look for opportunities to encourage teachers to work together during the process. They will also need to provide the correct mixture of encouragement, pressure and support to facilitate change. Beyond that work on an individual basis will need to relate to the overall aims and 'mission' of the school. Fairly recently another North American perspective on the conduct of the appraisal process was provided by the work of the Joint Committee on Standards for Educational Evaluation, chaired by D. L. Stufflebeam. The Joint Committee offered a series of guidelines for successful and acceptable appraisal. These included recommendations to review, recognize and build on areas of strength and to solicit the appraisee's suggestions for improving performance. Further, the committee drew attention to the practical details of follow-up, recommending follow-up conferences between the appraisee and appropriate support personnel, and help to the appraisee in the form of such things as resources and release time.

While some of the Joint Committee's advice reflects the particular traditions of appraisal in North America, it nevertheless draws attention to the importance of managing the appraisal process, particularly at the follow-up stage.

But all this is easier said than done. In effect, for development to follow from appraisal, changes are needed in the way individuals think and act. Such changes involve new learning and are not necessarily accomplished quickly nor without a certain amount of anxiety. Clearly in such situations proper support is needed, support provided to some extent by encouraging collaboration between colleagues and in part by continued interest and contact from the appraiser. Wise and his colleagues drew attention to these issues (1985, p. 69):

> To improve a teacher's performance, the school system must enlist the teacher's cooperation, motivate him (or her), and guide him through steps needed for improvement to occur. For the individual, improvement relies on the development of two important conditions: (1) the knowledge that a course of action is correct and (2) a sense of empowerment or efficacy, that is, a perception that pursuing a given course of action is both worthwhile and possible.
>
> Most teacher evaluation processes identify effective teaching without addressing the question of how to change teaching behaviour. The initiators of such processes assume that once they have discovered what ought to be done, teachers will naturally know what to do and will do it. Fenstermacher argues, however, that: 'if our purpose and intent are to change the practices of those who teach, it is necessary to come to grips with the subjectively reasonable beliefs of teachers' (1978, p. 174). This means creating internally verifiable knowledge rather than imposing rules of behaviour. It assumes, first, that teachers are rational professionals who make judgments and carry out decisions in an uncertain, complex environment and, second, that teachers' behaviour is guided by their thoughts, judgments, and decisions. Thus, behaviour change requires transformation of belief structures and knowledge in a manner that allows for situation-specific applications.

In other words those responsible for managing change need to resist the temptation to act on an overly rational conception of human behaviour. They need to give those involved an appropriate mixture of encouragement and pressure to assist them in their learning.

Appraisal is currently an innovation and will remain so for some time. Further, it is being introduced alongside other innovations. Our argument is that if effective change and development are to occur as a consequence of appraisal these implications for individual change need to be understood and incorporated into the planning processes.

TARGET SETTING

In this chapter we have so far considered some of the consequences for the individual teacher of being involved in innovation. We now consider some of the technical questions relating to appraisal target setting and the management of the follow-up phase of the process. We believe attention to these factors can facilitate the type of personal change processes we have been discussing.

We have already noted the advice given in the literature on the need to ensure that the appraisee participates at the appraisal interview in the planning of follow-up targets and activities. Both appraiser and appraisee need to check with each other their understanding of what has been proposed during the interview and set down targets in the form of a written action plan. Such an action plan would indicate the target, how and when it will be achieved, and criteria for judging successful accomplishment. It would also indicate support, timing and monitoring procedures.

The point has also been made fairly frequently that individual targets need to be set in the context of the overall plan and aims of the organization. In essence appraisal provides an important opportunity for harmonizing individual and organizational aims. In this respect appraisal is part of the planning strategy of the organization. With the advent of school development plans this link should become clearer. Indeed appraisal could serve to diagnose and review aspects of work in the school to enable the construction of a plan. Appraisal could also be a means of evaluating how well the plan is working. Together appraisal and school development plans provide the opportunity to strengthen leadership in schools in terms of 'motivating individuals to pursue overall organisational goals . . . and harnessing and mediating individuals' own goals and needs' (Morgan and Turner, 1976, p. 26).

We should like now to develop further the way we see the relationship between school development plans and the appraisal of individuals. Emerging practice in the area of school development plans suggests that work on them follows a cycle of review or audit, making or constructing the plan and implementing and evaluating the plan (see Figure 5.1).

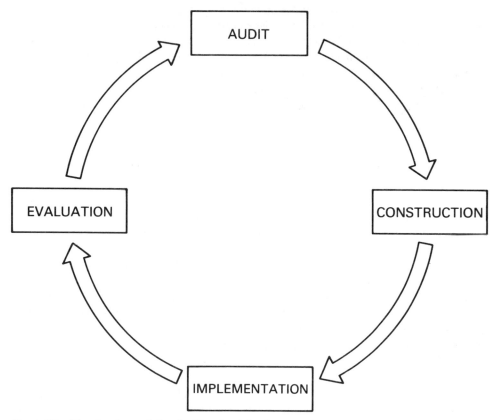

Figure 5.1   *The planning cycle involved in school development plans*
Source: Hargreaves *et al.* (1989)

Furthermore, although we have chosen to illustrate the process diagrammatically, we do not expect it to operate in so neat and direct a fashion. In practice, we would expect schools to move between the stages in different ways and at varying paces depending on issues under consideration.

At the review or audit stage, schools are preparing for planning. At this stage those involved review a range of aspects of school work in the light of school aims and philosophy, the environmental and general educational context and the demands of local and central government. From such a review or audit – and we prefer the term 'audit' as it draws attention to the need to plan within financial constraints – comes the identification of priorities and strategies for development.

We see appraisal as helpful to these first two stages of the planning process in a number of ways. First, it serves a diagnostic purpose in identifying areas for development. If such areas emerge repeatedly through the appraisal of several individuals, then they become matters for school concern. Second, the discussions involved in appraisal allow individuals to raise issues for broader consideration.

Once schools have formulated their development plans, they move to the twin processes of implementing and evaluating them. At these stages appraisal also appears helpful. Through appraisal those in positions of management can monitor aspects of the plan. Furthermore, appraisal, carried out in the ways suggested in this book, provides teachers and headteachers with support in attempting change. The collaborative and constructive model of appraisal we have recommended has much to offer here.

At the heart of the points made about the links between school development plans and appraisal is a belief that both of these involve harmonizing the needs and aims of the individual with those of the school. If the processes are at odds or not planned coherently, then the direction and cohesiveness of schools will suffer. But if both processes are seen as complementary, then combined they offer a major opportunity for school improvement and individual development.

The link between appraisal and school development plans provides the context in which to consider the range of advice on target or goal setting that is available. Goal setting is one of a number of motivation theories and has influenced the management by objectives approach. Locke makes the following claims for the usefulness of the goal-setting approach to motivation: 'goal-setting is simply the most directly useful motivational approach in a managerial context, since goals are the most immediate regulators of human action and are more easily modified than values or subconscious premises' (in Steers and Porter, 1983, p. 88).

Goal setting is seen as motivating in itself, as is the sense of striving towards a goal. According to Locke, goals need to be specific, challenging and accepted and seen as attainable by the person involved. Management by objectives approaches based on goal setting have typically involved meetings to set, review and monitor targets. There is however some disagreement as to what extent the setting of goals is important in comparison with other aspects of management, such as increased personal interaction, which typically accompany this process. Nevertheless, Cooper and Makin feel confident in advising people to 'set clear and moderately difficult goals that are accepted by the person concerned' (1984, p. 114). The popularity of objective setting and target setting in the UK has increased over recent years due to a number of factors. First, the DES requirement for schools to be more precise about their aims and objectives has created an appropriate context. Second, the increase of management training for senior staff and the availability of accessible literature, such as the writing of Trethowan, has done much to popularize the approach. Sometimes the training has resulted in review or appraisal schemes. It has also served to increase familiarity with advice on target setting, that targets should be

- specific;
- measurable;
- attainable;

- relevant;
- time-related.

It is important for appraisers and appraisees to consider these points when setting targets during appraisal. In particular the opportunity provided by appraisal for harmonizing individual and school planning should be kept in mind.

APPRAISAL AND DEVELOPMENT – THE PILOT STUDY EXPERIENCE

We have referred in detail already to experience from the School Teacher Appraisal Pilot Study of the developmental potential of the earlier stages of the appraisal process. It is perhaps appropriate simply to review this at this point. We were much encouraged, for example, by the emphasis given to self-appraisal and to the way other aspects of the process were set up so as to promote reflection. The inclusion of an element of peer observation in the process and the conceptualization of classroom observation as 'teaching analysis' or the interview as a 'professional dialogue' helped to turn a developmental philosophy into reality. All these strategies provide examples of a sensitivity to how teachers learn and interact.

The pilot study also saw an attempt to get maximum benefit from the follow-up stage, by drawing attention to what happened at the interview in terms of target setting.

The thinking referred to here can be seen in some of the advice given to teachers in the School Teacher Appraisal Pilot Study. For example, the following advice from Suffolk LEA relates to successful target setting:

Targets should:

be stated in clear, unambiguous language;

be few in number (2–5) depending on complexity;

be measurable or observable;

be challenging;

be realistic and attainable;

be job-orientated and relate to improved competence;

be related to, and consistent with, the philosophy of the school and the LEA;

include an 'action plan' with steps for implementation;

include some statement of what is considered to be an acceptable performance;

be discussed at intervals during the year by the parties concerned and modified if necessary;

be monitored.

The LEA also offered advice on the source of possible targets, providing a useful checklist to consider:

Source of Targets (derived through discussion with the appraiser):

1 The job description and the responsibilities associated with the job;

2 Criteria listed on the appraisal forms;

3 Teaching performance;

4 The last appraisal summary;

5 School targets;

6   Departmental targets;

7   LEA targets;

8   Targets set in a previous year;

9   Self-appraisal.

(Suffolk LEA, 1988a, pp. 17–18)

During the course of the School Teacher Appraisal Pilot Study we found a range of targets being set, which included those noted in the evaluation report:

(i)   classroom strategies e.g. to make changes in the organisation of the classroom, grouping pupils in a different way or developing a particular teaching strategy such as the introduction of a greater amount of computer based work;

(ii) school performance e.g. to carry out an additional responsibility such as taking charge of a cross-curricular initiative or taking on a coordination role;

(iii) career development e.g. to take on greater management responsibility within the school, or to go on a management course with a view to the next career move.

Most participants produced both long- and short-term targets. A number have reported a difficulty in setting clear and specific targets. The participants have, on the whole, kept to six or less, with a mix of long- and short-term targets related to classroom, school and career objectives.

(Bradley *et al.*, 1989)

The School Teacher Appraisal Pilot Study experience showed the importance of setting clear and specific targets against a timetable. It also demonstrated the need for clarity over responsibility for follow-up and for monitoring progress on targets. There was also a tendency, where target setting was not spotlighted in training, for targets to be vague and unspecific. In that situation the momentum of the process tended to be reduced. Often those who had gone through the experience were determined to be more specific over target setting during the next round of appraisal. It also became clear that in large schools systems were necessary for co-ordinating the target setting carried out by a team of appraisers. It was a question not only of co-ordinating staff development needs, but also of maintaining consistency and monitoring across the team.

What also became clear was the range of benefits teachers experienced as a result of appraisal. These benefits arose both during the process itself and as a result of target-setting. As we have noted already, frequently appraisal served to prompt reflection and greater self-awareness. It was also often an opportunity for receiving reassurance, recognition or praise. In these ways it served to boost confidence and morale. Teachers typically emerged from the process with a broader view of INSET and felt their INSET needs had been identified more precisely. Often the collaborative activities arising from appraisal were themselves viewed as a form of INSET. In terms of career development, appraisal tended to focus teachers' thinking on career aims and provide a chance to discuss appropriate strategies for career progression. Appraisal also typically served to improve communication in schools, leading to a greater sense of coherence and mutual understanding. It also encouraged teachers to work on and improve specific areas of their teaching to the benefit of their pupils. Where appraisal did not prove so beneficial this tended to be due to one of the following factors, which were identified in the CIE Evaluation Report.

Factors limiting the impact of appraisal

We can identify a number of factors which people believe threaten the impact of appraisal. These include:

- lack of appropriate training or a gap between training and appraisal;
- having an appraiser you don't have confidence in;
- failure to understand the process;
- interruptions to classroom observation or to the interview;
- delays in the process, for example in giving feedback, or writing up an appraisal statement;
- too 'cosy' an appraisal;
- vague targets;
- lack of attention to monitoring targets or follow-up;
- uncertainty over the availability of resources for follow-up;
- lack of commitment from the headteacher;
- pressure of other concerns and innovations;
- a fear that some people are not very good at 'selling' themselves.

(Bradley *et al.*, 1989, p. 63)

We also noted that teachers associated the following factors with successful appraisal:

Appraisal appears in general to work well if:

- the school has an open climate, where teachers are ready to discuss their work;
- suitable training has been provided for both appraisers and appraisees;
- the head is committed to the process;
- both appraisers and appraisees are clear about their responsibilities and understand the scheme;
- the process is well presented and well managed by the head or by an appraisal coordinator;
- there is previous experience of appraisal or a deliberate implementation strategy;
- professional relationships are good.

(Bradley *et al.*, 1989, pp. 63–4)

SUMMARY OF KEY POINTS

The factors outlined here serve to introduce the conclusion to this chapter. What appear particularly important are that:

1   Each stage of the appraisal process needs to be conducted so as to lead to development.

2   The implications for teachers of being involved in change and learning need to be considered.

3   The appraisal interview needs to be a two-way process in which both parties determine action plans for the future and clarify what is to happen.

4   Targets set need to be realistic, attainable, time-bound, monitored and supported.

5   As well as leading to work in specific target areas, appraisal can lead to broader, less tangible benefits, such as greater self-awareness or improved morale; in other words the outcomes of appraisal vary in their cost implications. Important benefits can be inexpensive.

6   Appraisal needs to be related to school aims and developments. In particular the appraisal process needs to be fitted into the rhythms and patterns of the school calendar. The process of appraisal can be further tied into the school's needs if areas of focus are selected, at least partly, from school priority issues.

   What is called for is a vision within the school of how school (and departmental) review, appraisal and school development plans can combine.

7   Appraisal targets need to be set within the parameters of available resources and strategies considered in the light of their cost-effectiveness: in particular it is a question of tying the appraisal process into support structures and into budgetary planning.

8   To achieve the benefits in terms of individual and school development we have referred to, appraisal needs to have time and energy devoted to it: it is perhaps a truism to say that the outcome depends on the quality of the process.

Chapter 6

Headteacher Appraisal

We have argued in previous chapters that if appraisal is to contribute significantly to organizational and individual development, rather than subside into a narrow 'checking' exercise aimed at guaranteeing minimum standards, then it must incorporate those processes which stimulate the pursuit of excellence. In the case of headteacher appraisal, at least three factors seem crucial to the creation of suitable conditions.

First, the recognition that appraisal is above all a *dialogue*, between superior and subordinate, about goals, priorities, methods and opportunities. A major outcome of the process should be the appraisee's increased awareness of how, by directing his/her future effort, it is possible to contribute to organizational development through achieving personal goals, and conversely, to achieve personal goals through contributing to organizational development.

Second, and following from this, the appraiser will need detailed knowledge of both the organization – its culture and values, its structures and roles – and the individual – his/her specific responsibilities and tasks and their relationships with those of others, and of the particular pattern of strengths and weaknesses the individual currently possesses in relation to the requirements of the job. It is this knowledge which enables constructive analysis of current performance to be carried out. This in turn informs planning and target setting for the future, and helps appraisers and appraisees jointly to identify the programme for support and personal development most appropriate to the longer-term growth of organization and individual.

Third, the appraiser will need to be in position to influence the current structure of roles and responsibilities, and provide those opportunities for development which have been mutually agreed as appropriate. This enables the organization to benefit from the outcomes of the appraisal process and helps to create a dynamic organizational culture in which structured personal development contributes both to increased levels of organizational performance and to increased levels of individual competence and satisfaction.

While difficult to secure, these circumstances are not impossible in the case of teacher appraisal, though it can be anticipated that schools will take a number of years to move towards them. Headteachers, however, are in a rather different position, since the facility to build in these factors would seem to rely on a stronger and very much more direct link between headteachers and their employing authorities than has previously been the norm.

This was, in part, acknowledged in *Those Having Torches*:

> If the appraisal of headteachers is to be developmental and constructive then the headteacher's 'line manager' must be clearly defined. 'Line managers' are expected to be people who *know* the subordinate's work well and who are also intimately acquainted with the context in which that work is carried out.
> (Suffolk Education Dept, 1985)

But whilst satisfying the first two criteria referred to earlier, this still leaves the question of responsibility for organizing (and resourcing) any follow-up activity unresolved. This is not to criticize the 'Torches' team, as how that issue can best be approached remains immensely problematic. But in looking at headteachers' appraisal it needs to be clear from the outset that though much of the ACAS document implied parity between teacher and headteacher appraisal, in practice this may be difficult to realize, and a number of issues apparently resolved in teacher appraisal will need to be considered again in the particular context in which headteachers work.

WHY APPRAISE HEADTEACHERS?

The case for the appraising of headteachers has been argued from a number of perspectives, varying from the belief in some quarters that the head's right to engage in teacher appraisal depends on his/her willingness to take part in a similar process, to the assertion that the appraisal of headteachers is a legitimate management responsibility of the LEA. The most frequently mentioned arguments include the following.

Parity

There is a strong feeling (which extends to headteachers themselves) that a headteacher's right to participate in the appraisal of teachers will stem from the headteacher's willingness to be appraised in turn. This is supported by the notion that the headteacher's credibility within teacher appraisal will also hinge on personal involvement and experience as an appraisee. Though there is no hard evidence to support this view, it is one which has strong emotional support from many teachers, and so could be an important factor in determining school climate and readiness for appraisal. Whilst accepting then, the force of this argument, it may nevertheless be worthwhile to underline that the need for fairness or equity between the treatment of headteachers and teachers does not necessarily imply an identical series of activities or length of appraisal cycle.

Isolation

Headteachers as a group have enjoyed little in the way of formal support structures or systems from LEAs. Recent years have seen significant increases in the number of headteachers seeking early retirement, and the recent NAHT survey (Kelly, 1988) indicates that headteachers anticipate increasing pressure and job-related stress in the future. (More than a third anticipated stress from appraisal itself!) Though the professional isolation of the headteacher is only one of the factors causing stress, it also makes it more difficult for headteachers to cope with stress from other sources. Clearly, appraisal, and the dialogue which comes with it, offers to headteachers an opportunity to share their anxieties and problems, as well as their hopes and plans, with an informed 'outsider' in a constructive and supportive context. The morale (in most cases) and mental health (in some) of headteachers can therefore be greatly reinforced through appraisal.

School Development

The lack of support for headteachers at a personal level frequently extends to professional matters too. The difficulty many headteachers are currently experiencing in producing school development plans is one example of the gap which exists between school and LEA, and of the problem headteachers have in bridging that gap without professional advice and support. Schools are also on the threshold of an era of increased devolution, which is likely to further weaken LEA/school mutuality. There is, as never before, a vital need at school level to produce high-quality, whole-school development plans, and to communicate these to the staff –

Margaret Madden (LEAP I, 1989) has described this as the need to evolve and project a 'mental vision' of what the school will be. The evolution of this 'mental vision', which will become the basis for establishing priorities and for decision making within the school, can be greatly supported by the review and target setting elements of the appraisal process, and the detail of the vision considerably sharpened and focused through the appraisal dialogue.

Headteacher Development

Though the last five years have seen a significant increase in the number of headteachers who are offered training/development opportunities, this remains a problematic area. Ann Jones summarized this:

> Very few heads have been selected for their qualities of leadership in troubled times, their ability to resolve conflict or to straddle uncomfortable polarities, nor, by and large, have they been trained in these skills, even though training is possible.
>
> (Jones, 1987)

All too often, where training opportunities have been available these have not been targeted on specific, identified needs, but advertised in the LEA's INSET programme inviting those interested to apply. As a consequence, even the modest amount of training which has gone on has had a poorer return for LEA and school than should be possible if the matching of individual headteachers with specific training opportunities is managed in a systematic way. Appraisal provides a vehicle for, at least, alerting headteachers to their own priorities and thus helping them to make more informed decisions themselves about the development opportunities available. It may also provide the LEA with a profile of headteachers' needs which can influence the balance of provision and improve responsiveness.

Resource Allocation

Often, headteachers feel that school development is constrained by lack of resources. Sometimes this resource shortage is seen as rendering the implementation of LEA policies or programmes impossible. Conversely, it sometimes appears that the LEA makes resources available without any clear expectations of what those resources will add to or maintain in the school. Perhaps, if appropriate communication procedures could be agreed, the outcomes of headteachers' appraisals could directly influence the pattern of resourcing from the LEA in specific areas. Similarly, though this will take some time to test out, it may be that some method of communicating outcomes to school governors would facilitate changes in the pattern of resources within the school.

WHO SHOULD APPRAISE HEADTEACHERS?

The ACAS agreement (ACAS, 1986) stated that:

> The appraisal of Headteachers will be the responsibility of the Chief Education Officer who shall appoint as appraiser an appropriate person with relevant experience as a Headteacher, who will be required to consult with the designated Inspector responsible for the school, and the designated Education Officer.

Though this implies that LEA structures will feature a pastoral attachment of particular inspectors to particular schools (which is by no means the case in all LEAs) and some system of 'area' responsibility amongst officers, which tends to be a function of LEA size rather than a uniform pattern of organization, no further advice on who should appraise headteachers is contained in the ACAS agreement.

The Suffolk appraisal team (Suffolk Education Dept, 1987) underlines and develops this approach:

> The appraisal of headteachers is a complex process best tackled by a team approach. Familiarity with the school and wider LEA practices is essential.
>
> The process should be professionally conducted and be the responsibility of the Chief Education Officer.
>
> The appraisal team should contain an appointed appraiser, with relevant experience as a headteacher who should coordinate both the process and the range of professional input. No one individual is likely to have the range of experience and background knowledge demanded by the process.

The team also emphasized the importance headteachers' self-appraisal will have in the overall process.

The majority of developmental work on headteachers' appraisal has followed these three strands – though the balance and emphases between them have varied

- input from 'above' (or outside the school);

- input from a peer headteacher (who has done some, albeit limited, data collection inside the school); and

- input from the appraisee him/herself.

In this model, the LEA officer attempts to fulfil the role of 'line manager' to the headteacher, and the transactions between the co-ordinator and the appraisee headteacher mirror those which take place inside school for the appraisal of teachers, though the assumptions the parties bring to the process may be somewhat different.

Others have argued for a more direct involvement of subordinates in the process of headteacher appraisal. Yates, for example, suggests that: 'The involvement of teachers in the appraisal of the headteacher can provide an opportunity for extending the professional development of all those involved' (Yates, in Bunnell, 1987). In this approach the role of outsiders is seen as facilitative rather than co-ordinating: 'The use of an experienced outsider facilitator may open up self-appraisal and feedback for staff since he or she has no managerial connection with the headteacher or staff' (Yates, in Bunnell, 1987).

Though this 'school-centred' approach presents some interesting possibilities, it does not reflect the growing demand for external accountability, and seems unlikely to be incorporated in national or LEA approaches in the foreseeable future.

In the end the success of headteacher appraisal will depend on the *qualities of the individuals* who are to be the appraisers rather than the system of identifying these individuals, though an 'inappropriate' method of selection may guarantee failure. So in planning for headteacher appraisal it is necessary to remember that whilst the 'imposition' of an appraiser who does not have what the appraisee considers relevant experience may sour the process from the outset, simply ensuring that all appraisers have had relevant experience will not be sufficient. The following points may provide a useful starting point, by listing some key issues for consideration.

Credibility: Appraisers will need to be credible to heads yet also credible to other interested parties including 'the observer on the top deck of the Clapham omnibus' (Suffolk Education Dept, 1987, p. 6).

Consistency: The decision on who appraises heads cannot be seen in isolation from who appraises teachers. The implications of adopting a line management model for teacher appraisal alongside peer appraisal for heads need to be considered. A call for subordinate appraisal of heads, for example, cannot be seen in isolation from subordinate appraisal of teachers.

Competence: The question here is – do appraisers have sufficient knowledge and awareness of the head's job to be in a position to offer adequate diagnosis and support?

Capability: Given the commitment in the ACAS principles to following up appraisal, and evidence from industry that schemes failing in this respect lose credibility, are appraisers in a position to guarantee delivery of identified needs for in-service development?

To this list the issue of governor involvement could usefully be added. The ACAS agreement preceded both the 1986 and 1988 Education Acts, which have significantly altered in balance the relationship between school governors and the LEA. Indeed, with the introduction of local management of schools (LMS), school governing bodies will become the direct employers of staff in a majority of schools. It may reasonably be asked how any system of appraisal, however 'professional', can effectively exclude employers. At minimum it seems likely that the head-teacher appraisal systems will need to give some indication of how governors should be involved in the appraisal of headteachers, both as sources of data about the school and the headteacher's performance, and as the responsible body to whom some formal report of the appraisal process and its outcomes needs to be made.

WHAT SHOULD HEADTEACHERS' APPRAISAL INVOLVE?

There is a broad acceptance that the process of headteacher appraisal should, by and large, parallel the appraisal of teachers. Thus a similar series of stages can be identified, though there may need to be a modification of the activities at the various stages to reflect the different role and emphasis within the headteacher's job. A number of suggested formats for these stages are now available, for example the Somerset LEA's *Head Light* (1988b), Suffolk LEA's *Notes of Guidance for Headteacher Appraisal* (1988b) and Salford LEA's *Headteacher Appraisal Information* (1989).

Though the number of distinct components suggested and the order in which they should (ideally) be carried out varies slightly between the various schemes, there is general agreement that a number of activities are essential following the identification of appraisers for the particular headteacher. As Figure 6.1 indicates, some of these activities are specific to appraisee, while others are shared.

Familiarization

Appraiser(s) will need to be aware of the context in which the school operates, and the policies, structure and style of operation of the school itself. There will therefore be a requirement for a process of familiarization during which appraisers prepare for the initial review meeting with the headteacher. This preparation would include consideration of current national and local policies relevant to the context in which the school functions, as well as assimilation of information about current school policies and practices. The range of background data on the

69

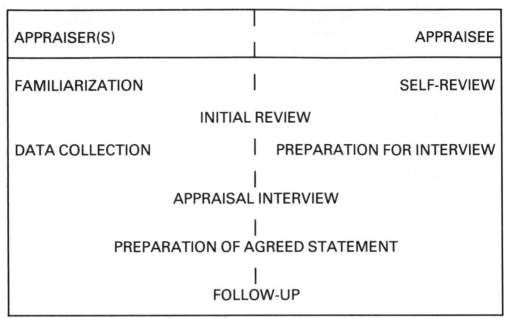

APPRAISER(S)		APPRAISEE
FAMILIARIZATION		SELF-REVIEW
	INITIAL REVIEW	
DATA COLLECTION		PREPARATION FOR INTERVIEW
	APPRAISAL INTERVIEW	
	PREPARATION OF AGREED STATEMENT	
	FOLLOW-UP	

Figure 6.1   *The process of headteacher appraisal*

school which could be relevant here is vast, so some selection is likely to be necessary. However, information on curriculum, staffing, management and administrative practices will be essential. It is difficult to see how appraisers can obtain this information without the co-operation of the headteacher, who will need to provide a package of relevant documents to assist the assimilation process.

Self-review

Whilst the appraisers are becoming familiar with the school, headteachers will also need to prepare for the initial review. This meeting will be most fruitful if the headteacher has already undertaken some form of self-appraisal, and is willing to share the outcome of this process with the appraiser(s). Many headteachers find self-review is assisted by the use of checklists or pro formas, though others feel that 'a blank sheet of paper' is the most productive approach. The method of self-review is probably best left to the individual, though all headteachers should be urged to undertake some form of self-assessment before the initial review meeting.

Initial Review

The initial review meeting should serve three purposes. First, informed by the familiarization and self-review processes, it should enable appraiser(s) and headteachers to take stock of the school's current position and the headteacher's feelings about this position. It should also enable the headteacher to take stock of his/her role within the school, and to reflect upon his/her recent performance in general terms.

Second, it should provide the opportunity to agree areas of focus for that particular appraisal cycle. In agreeing these areas it will be important to consider any national or LEA initiatives that will have a bearing on the head's role during the review period, as well as those areas of current performance where the head feels that particular problems or opportunities present themselves. It will also be important to identify as precisely as possible those aspects of the *headteacher*'s behaviour and performance which are to be looked at, rather than identifying areas of performance within the school. There may be occasions, for example in the case of recently appointed headteachers, where it is thought desirable to consider a wide range of the headteacher's functions, but the available evidence suggests that more usually it will be beneficial to focus on a limited number of specific areas, so that the exercise does not become too superficial. (As the appraisal cycles continue, it may be necessary to build in some means of ensuring that the areas of focus are varied so that significant aspects of the headteacher's role are not consistently overlooked.)

Third, it should lead to clear agreement about what sorts of data appraisers will need to collect in order to shed light on the headteacher's performance in the agreed areas, and by what methods and from whom this data will be collected. This is potentially a highly sensitive area, and the 'Code of Practice for Data Collection' appended to the National Steering Group Report (NSG, 1989) is likely to provide helpful guidance on this issue to all those involved in data collection activities (see Appendix 2).

Data Collection

Though the specific data collected will depend upon the agreed areas of focus, a number of likely sources suggest themselves:

1 Published data relating to policies, work and achievements of the school.

2 LEA officers (including inspectors and advisers) who are able to provide insights into the particular areas of headteacher performance under review.

3 Governors, parents and other non-staff members of the school community, where the views of such groups/individuals are relevant to the area(s) under review.

4 Members of the teaching staff within the school.

5 Task observation of the headteacher at work, including, where teaching has been identified as a major focus, classroom observation.

It will be important to concentrate data collection activities upon the agreed areas of focus – no impression should be created that the identification of appraisers for headteachers implies a general invitation to groups or individuals to funnel their comments or complaints about the headteacher to the appraiser in the expectation that the appraiser will somehow introduce these into the agenda.

It will also be necessary to ensure that data collection activities are properly planned and (where more than one appraiser is involved) co-ordinated. It may well be necessary therefore for the appraisers (where more than one is involved) to meet to consider the data which has been collected, to agree on what is relevant and needs to be fed into the appraisal dialogue, and to plan generally for the appraisal interview.

Preparation (by the Appraisee Headteacher) for the Appraisal Interview

It is desirable that headteachers, having had the initial review meeting, do not then perceive their role as one of waiting until the appraiser has gathered information on the agreed areas of focus, and then turning up for the interview to receive some kind of 'report'. The appraiser collects data in order to service a more meaningful and constructive dialogue than would otherwise be possible. Headteachers will need to undertake parallel preparations for the interview in order to achieve maximum benefit. This implies that headteachers will think very carefully about their behaviour and performance in the areas of focus. For example, they might try to identify any decisions they have taken within those areas, and consider how and why the decision was taken, and the degree to which it has proved effective. It may also be instructive to reconsider alternatives that were rejected, and again to apply the benefits of hindsight. The emphasis should be on exploring areas of performance with a view to increasing understanding both of the requirements of the situation and of the headteacher's influence, intended and unintended, on subsequent events. This will help headteachers to come to the appraisal interview ready to discuss not only what they have done but also *why*, and encourage an atmosphere in which headteachers can be constructively self-critical without feeling the need to defend, rather than explain, their actions.

A second area where headteachers could usefully give some thought concerns targets for the coming review period. What are the opportunities for action? How can these be prioritized, what action from the headteacher, and from others, will be necessary? What resources will be involved? Above all, headteachers should view this period as an opportunity to prepare themselves for formal professional dialogue in which they will have the opportunity to review previous performance and experiences as learning opportunities and benefit from the additional perception and insights that the appraisers can provide.

The Interview

The interview itself should be similar in purpose to teacher appraisal interviews, which are discussed in some detail in Chapter 4. There are, however, one or two differences which perhaps need mention. It is likely, for example, that there will be more than one appraiser present, so it is necessary that the appraisers, as part of their preparation, have agreed a strategy for conducting the interview, and the appraisee headteacher is informed of how the various stages of the interview will be handled and who will lead the discussion. Similarly, there may need to be agreement about who will keep note of the discussion.

Target setting may also prove more difficult – many headteachers' 'targets' could be long term. Where targets are predominantly long term it will be important to identify 'indicators' which can provide interim progress reports (the relationship between short-term goals and achievement levels is well established).

Preparation of the Agreed Statement

Again, the procedures relating to the preparation of agreed statements for teacher appraisal (see Chapter 4) will generally apply, though in the case of headteachers it seems reasonable to assume that a copy of the agreed statement should be available to the Chief Education Officer. This would enable any common needs arising from headteacher appraisal to be identified, and thus create an opportunity for a directed LEA response.

There is then the issue of school governing bodies. It is clear that there will need to be some way of assuring governing bodies that the appraisal of the headteacher has been properly conducted. It is less clear whether, beyond that, there needs to be some method of governor access to the agreed statement, or at least parts of this. One possibility would be a requirement that in all cases an 'edited' version of the agreed statement subsequently be produced for the governing body. A second would be to inform governors of the headteacher's agreed targets. This is a very difficult area in which to legislate – in practice it is likely that the extent to which governors are informed about the outcomes of headteacher appraisal will vary according to the quality of relationships which exist between headteachers and their governing bodies. At minimum, some method of informing governors of 'outcomes' which will require their agreement in order to proceed is necessary. What else (if anything) is to be communicated to governors, can probably best be determined by appraisers and appraisee at the point when the agreed statement is being produced.

Follow-up

Two sorts of follow-up are vital if appraisal is to retain credibility as a worthwhile and developmental process. The first, follow-up action by others to support the appraisee in pursuing the agreed targets, is particularly problematic in the case of headteachers and is discussed in more detail later in this chapter. The second, follow-up by the appraiser him/herself will need to be monitored in the case of headteachers as it will with teachers. So the appraisers will not have completed their task once the agreed statement has been produced, but will retain a continuing responsibility to the appraisee, and in particular will need to identify a timetable for reviewing progress in those areas where the appraisee has identified targets or is committed to action. This will provide for continuity between appraisal cycles, as well as helping the appraisee head to focus on those areas which have been identified as priorities for action.

WHEN SHOULD HEADTEACHER APPRAISAL TAKE PLACE?

The timing of headteachers' appraisal poses two questions – over what period of time should the appraisal of a headteacher be spread, and how far apart should the individual appraisals be? The answers to these questions should be consistent with the ACAS principle: 'The Working Group understands appraisal not as a series of perfunctory periodic events, but as a continuous and systematic process intended to help teachers with their professional development . . . ' (ACAS, 1986).

The period of time over which the appraisal process is spread is most influenced by the requirement for data gathering. In the case of headteachers, this process of collection will in turn be influenced by who the appraisers are. If, as seems likely, a practising headteacher is involved, then the need to fit these demands into an already crowded schedule will be an important consideration. Nevertheless, the process of data collection must not become so protracted that it becomes disjointed. It is desirable, therefore, that data gathering be carried out over not more than one school term. If the process of familiarization is added to the front of this and time is allocated between the various subsequent stages to ensure opportunity for thought and reflection then it may well take as long as six months to complete any one appraisal cycle – excluding the follow-up review meeting. The timing of the review meeting needs to be determined in relation to the nature of the targets to be followed up, and the interval between cycles.

It is possible to make a case for different levels of interval between cycles, depending on which factors are considered most important. Where the LEA is mindful of the costs of headteacher appraisal and the logistical difficulties of introducing and maintaining the scheme, a three-year interval is clearly attractive. This could be supported by reference to the nature of the headteacher's job, and the sorts of decisions headteachers are required to make, many of which cannot properly be evaluated until several years have elapsed (see Patterson, 1978, for an account of the 'time span of discretion' approach to decision making). Where the emphasis is on establishing a continuous dialogue or providing headteachers and teachers within appraisal with similar schedules, this will lead to the major consideration being the length of interval between teacher appraisals. This is reflected in the National Steering Group Report (NSG, 1989), which proposes a two-year interval between appraisals for teachers and headteachers alike. Should this become the national model, then the follow-up/review meeting would probably need to be initiated in the year following the appraisal process, in order to provide for some continuity into the next cycle, whilst allowing 12 months before reviewing progress in agreed target areas.

HOW SHOULD HEADTEACHER APPRAISAL BE FOLLOWED UP?

It is necessary to return to the question of how any targets emerging from headteacher appraisal requiring supporting action from others can best be followed up. As noted earlier, there is no clear equivalent to the 'line manager' for headteachers. The tradition of headteacher autonomy, coupled with the current reforms, has created an uncertain partnership between headteachers, governors and LEAs, but it will be necessary nevertheless to examine the particular responsibilities of the various partners. Where follow-up action requires *new* resources, then that would seem to be the responsibility of the LEA (though of course, LEAs will decreasingly have resources available to command).

Where follow-up requires a change in existing patterns of resource use, that would seem to be a matter for the governors of the school to determine. However, in practice, matters are unlikely to be so straightforward. If the LEA resource required is, for example, assistance from advisers or curriculum development teams, it will probably in the end depend on the headteacher's ability to 'draw in' the relevant people. Similarly, whilst a decision to switch staffing resources from one area to another will require the approval of the governing body, the headteacher will most often be able to secure the necessary support by the way the case is presented. The main burden of pursuing the necessary follow-up activities will in all probability, therefore, remain with the headteacher, though, and importantly, the appraisal dialogue will provide the headteacher with an opportunity to discuss how best to go about this, and possibly helpful advice or suggestions. Headteachers can be supported in two ways. The LEA will be in a position to identify common issues and areas for development from the headteachers' agreed statements. It is important that the LEA respond positively to this information – perhaps by identifying a portion of the INSET budget which will be earmarked to fund outcomes arising from the appraisal of headteachers.

Appraisers, having been closely involved in the headteacher's analysis of self and of school, will evolve considerable shared understanding with headteachers. They will therefore be important sources of emotional, as well as possibly practical, support. This role should not be underestimated in times of great stress and pressure on headteachers at all levels within the system.

THE EXPERIENCE OF THE SCHOOL TEACHER APPRAISAL PILOT STUDY

A number of different models for headteacher appraisal were trialled in the pilot LEAs. Typically these models featured two appraisers, of whom at least one had headship experience, though the method of selecting suitable appraisers varied considerably between LEAs. In addition a number of different training strategies were employed both for appraisers and appraisees, but there was broad agreement that training is most effective when it is available on a continuing basis, is essentially practical in nature and interlocks with 'live' appraisal experience. (For a fuller account of these issues see the evaluation report: Bradley *et al.*, 1989.)

Even at this early stage in the development of headteacher appraisal it was possible to identify some positive outcomes from the pilot schemes. For appraisees, for example, there was clear evidence that the headteacher's sense of isolation had been alleviated by the appraisal process. Similarly, many headteachers felt that the process had been a significant personal development experience. Appraisal also seemed to help headteachers to think about how the many different pressures and demands currently being placed upon schools could be managed and co-ordinated – in particular there seemed to be evidence of longer-term and more meaningful planning for school development.

Appraisers, too, felt that the process had been worth while – many described their involvement as appraisers as the most profound professional development experience they had undergone, and there was clearly the opportunity for transfer of ideas and approaches between the appraiser and the appraisee which could well have beneficial implications for the appraiser's school too. In a minority of cases appraisers were drawn from a different phase of education, and in these cases significant increases in understanding of the context and problems of this other phase were reported.

The pilot LEAs themselves gained valuable data from the process – clearer information on the felt needs of headteachers, a more accurate picture of the role headteachers felt that the LEA should play in support of schools, and an opportunity (in some instances) to improve communication between those LEA officers involved in the appraisal process and the appraiser and appraisee headteachers.

A number of meaningful issues which had not always been resolved satisfactorily also emerged. Among these were:

Credibility of Appraisers: The selection and training of suitable appraisers is seen as crucial to appraiser–appraisee relationship and to the value of the process.

Usefulness of the Headteacher's Job Description: In many cases the headteacher role was poorly defined and documented by the LEA; this created the additional problem of agreeing on a 'working definition' of headship during early stages.

Task Observation: Though task observation (including, where appropriate, classroom observation) had typically been carried out, appraisers were dubious about the value of this activity beyond gaining a general impression of the headteacher's style and approach. There was a feeling that specific training was required for specific observation activities if the process was to provide meaningful data for the appraisal interview.

Time Requirement: Many appraisers experienced a sense of guilt over the time they had devoted to appraising a colleague – there was a sense in which this could be interpreted as neglect of the appraiser's own school.

LEAs will need to do what they can to legitimize involvement as an appraiser within the range of headteacher tasks, as this problem will clearly be exacerbated by widespread adoption of appraisal: somewhere between a third and a half of all headteachers at any one time could potentially be appraisers.

Links between Appraisal and Other Review Processes: Many headteachers seemed confused about where appraisal, however worthwhile in itself, fitted in with other school review processes. In particular, it was felt that guidance on the relationships between the appraisal of headteachers, school self-review and school inspection would be helpful.

SUMMARY OF KEY POINTS

Headteacher appraisal should seek to create a dialogue between headteachers and their appraisers about goals, priorities, problems and opportunities. It can contribute to

- reducing the professional isolation of headteachers;

- stimulating individual development of both appraisee and appraiser;

- planning for school development;

- improved resource distribution and utilization at LEA and school levels;

- the creation of a climate conducive to meaningful teacher appraisal.

Those involved in the appraisal of a particular headteacher should include at least one person who has recent relevant experience as a headteacher within the appropriate phase of education. All those involved will need

- credibility – with those to be appraised and with the wider educational community;

- consistency in approach and judgement;

- competence to offer advice and support;

- capability – to ensure that appropriate follow-up takes place.

Though a number of different models for the appraisal process are possible the following stages should be included

- self-review, by the appraisee headteacher;

- initial review discussion – to agree areas of focus and procedures for data collection;

- data gathering by appraisers;

- appraisal interview, covering both recent performance and future targets;

- preparation of agreed statement;

- follow-up/review meeting(s).

Chapter 7

Training for Appraisal

The ACAS document states that 'all teachers should be trained to play their part in appraisal'. The availability of funding for appraisal training via the Local Evaluation Authority Training Grants Scheme (LEATGS) indicates the government's recognition that INSET support is a priority. This acknowledges that whilst teachers currently possess many of the necessary skills and currently engage in many of the processes which come together to create an appraisal system, the successful introduction of a formal scheme is unlikely to be achieved without the support of specific, targeted, INSET.

This chapter will consider how such support can be identified, planned for and delivered. It will take as its starting point the notion that any single-issue INSET programme, such as training for teacher appraisal, needs to be informed by a wider understanding of what makes for effective staff development. It will then attempt to set out the major issues confronting those planning for appraisal training and will draw upon the experiences of the teacher appraisal pilot schemes in seeking to establish general principles and approaches. Finally, it will consider the need to monitor training activity and to integrate it into the overall INSET strategy of the LEA.

DEVELOPING A TRAINING STRATEGY

There is an extensive literature concerning effective staff development in education. Most often this focuses on strategies to support changes in teaching behaviour (see, for example, Joyce and Showers, 1980, 1988; Hopkins, 1986) and some writers have looked in detail at the role of the training course in this context (see particularly Main, 1985; Rudduck, 1981). The consensus, however, suggests that the training course as such is perceived as having a limited (and decreasingly significant) role in shaping teacher development. Substantial change in teacher behaviour requires a closer integration of 'on' and 'off the job' experiences than the typical one-off training experience can achieve.

A number of themes which recur in the literature will need to be addressed by INSET planners if the training is to have a fundamental and enduring impact on actual teacher behaviour. These include:

1 A recognition of where the school and its teachers are starting from, and a commitment to help them to move forward from there, rather than simply describing to them where they are expected to move to.

2 A realistic assessment of the costs and benefits associated with the planned change, and a clear strategy for demonstrating that the costs are sustainable and will be justified by the benefits which follow.

3 An appreciation that change requires new knowledge and understanding as

well as skills, and that different methods and approaches will be required to satisfy these different stages of learning.

4 An understanding of the barriers to change and of training strategies which can be drawn on to eliminate these barriers and to assuage the inevitable (and justifiable) anxieties of teachers.

5 An ability to value teachers' current knowledge and experiences which are relevant to new activities, situations and encounters that appraisal will bring.

6 An appreciation of the need for support at and beyond the point of implementation, as the new activities associated with appraisal begin to be assimilated into the teachers' existing routines and therefore interact with and change these routines.

So it is important that those involved in designing training to support this major new initiative are not lured into seeing the initiative and, by extrapolation, the best method of promoting it, in isolation. From the outset some picture of how (and when) the focus for teacher development must shift away from central training activity and into the school is necessary.

Alongside this shift in focus will need to be an understanding that a range of training approaches will be needed. Joyce and Showers' findings concerning effective teacher learning are significant here, suggesting that a successful training strategy will have a number of components:

- presentation of theory or description of skill;

- modelling or demonstration of skills;

- practice in simulated and in school settings;

- structured and open-ended 'feedback' (information about performance);

- coaching for application.

(Joyce and Showers, 1980)

Training for appraisal, then, will need to offer a range of learning opportunities spread over a period of time and linked closely to implementation. One way of conceptualizing this process is provided by Likert (1967). His studies of organizational 'performance' in a range of organizational settings suggested that management was all too frequently preoccupied by the need to secure 'results' without identifying the sequence of variables which would lead to those 'results'. The model Likert derives from his studies of how people, and therefore organizations, change is simple yet enduringly instructive – results are determined by behaviour, behaviour stems from attitudes – therefore developing appropriate attitudes is a prerequisite to securing results.

In planning to introduce any new activity, therefore, such as the implementation of an effective appraisal scheme, it will be necessary to ensure that those involved are able to acquire appropriate attitudes (for example confidence, trust, willingness to experiment) and to develop the required behaviours (i.e. possess the appropriate skills). If quality and amount of information concerning the change is added to the beginning of this sequence, a three-stage model emerges.

STAGE 1   What do teachers need to know about appraisal?

STAGE 2   What do teachers need to feel about appraisal?

STAGE 3   What do teachers need to be able to do within appraisal?

Of course (like most models) this rather simplifies the problem and implies a linear relationship which is unlikely to be wholly sustained. Indeed, there are a number of writers who have argued that competence leads to commitment (see Joyce, 1990; Joyce and Showers, 1988; Guskey, 1986), which would suggest that Stage 3 should perhaps precede Stage 2. However, it seems reasonable to conclude that initially, at least, attitudes will be an important determinant of the rate of skill acquisition, though subsequently Stages 2 and 3 are likely to interact and to reinforce one another. The model is put forward therefore as one which can help to describe the way in which training needs to transfer *into* the school as development progresses away from a common informational base into a highly personalized learning experience. It can then be used to provide the skeleton for an LEA strategy (see Figure 7.1).

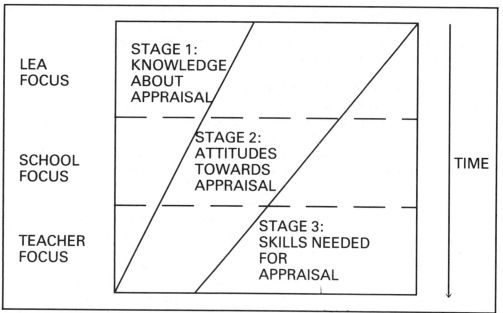

Figure 7.1   *Training for appraisal*

Stage 1: Knowledge about Appraisal

It is important that information about appraisal is high quality, consistent and (in terms of the training pattern) front-loaded. The LEA's particular scheme will obviously form the foundation for this aspect of the training, though it will be sensible to consider what form the national guidelines, which are promised, are likely to take. Clear documentation should be available, preferably in the same format, to all those involved, regardless of phase or seniority. Although inevitably there will be a continuing need to update teachers as schemes develop, and 'new' areas of knowledge needing attention will emerge as teachers embark upon the processes of appraisal, the major impact of information transfer needs to be felt before any activity takes place within the school.

Stage 2: Attitudes towards Appraisal

The need to develop and to maintain appropriate attitudes will persist throughout the training cycle. Attitudes will inevitably, in the first instance, be conditioned in part by the effectiveness of the selection and presentation of relevant information. In particular, teachers will need to be reassured about the LEA's commitment to appraisal as a developmental process, and confident that data generated from appraisal activity will be used constructively to inform the LEA's wider training strategy. However, the need to generate a climate of mutual trust in which professional dialogue can flourish will be most critical at the point where the school as a community begins to engage with the appraisal scheme. The emphasis here will be on how, within the training strategy, individual LEAs can support schools in developing a climate conducive to experimentation, growth and development. It will be necessary therefore to acknowledge the school as a separate culture, and to foster the development of appropriate relationships, commitment and mutuality within the school community. Since, for individual teachers this overall climate is a pre-condition for valid exchanges within the appraisal process rather than a guarantee that these will ensue, it is desirable that attention to attitudes be maintained by those organizing training activity as individual teachers begin to acquire personal experiences of the appraisal activities.

Stage 3: Skills needed for Appraisal

The appraisal process itself will bring with it the need for teachers to develop new skills, or at least the capacity to deploy existing skills in new situations. Though it is important from the outset (i.e. Stage 1) to identify what these skills are and how and where they will be required, it is difficult to develop them away from the 'real' situations. Inevitably, the major learning will stem from the accumulation of real experiences, and in this sense perhaps the whole of the first cycle of appraisal in any one school should be viewed initially as a training/development exercise. This is an important issue for trainers, as it is essential that time and opportunities are created at the implementation stage for teachers to discuss their experiences and to distil from them an understanding of those skills which underpin good practice. The combinations of skills which best fit the individual are likely to vary according to the different qualities and experiences of teachers. So it is desirable that there is at least some consensus within the school about which skills teachers will need to draw from, for example within the appraisal dialogues, or whilst undertaking classroom observation. Some discussion, then, about the relevant skills and how these can be developed and applied is desirable in Stage 2 of the training in order to produce a common framework and approach and to ensure that individualized competence does not become idiosyncratic.

ISSUES ARISING FROM TRAINING FOR APPRAISAL

Within this broad framework, there are a number of issues to which those planning appraisal training will need to pay attention at the various stages of the training effort.

As mentioned earlier, it is desirable that the initial stage of training adopt an LEA focus since it is important that there is a consistent message to teachers about the LEA's proposals and intentions. It would seem sensible also to draw on a limited number of trainers at this stage, to ensure continuity between training events and messages. It seems likely therefore that the LEA will wish to identify a training team to undertake this phase of the training who are essentially *outside* the school (though they may well be drawn from schools). Several factors will influence the effectiveness of this training team.

Credibility

Whether the trainers are practising teachers, other LEA staff or 'bought in' from outside the LEA, it is vital that they are perceived as 'credible', both in terms of their knowledge/experience of schools and their understanding of the appraisal process.

Quality and Amount of Information Available

It is important that teachers emerge from this first training experience with a clear understanding of two areas. First, the scope, purposes and implications of appraisal as a process (this could be termed 'awareness raising'). Second, the specific components, approaches and methods to be applied within the LEA scheme: understanding is more likely to grow and reflection more likely to contribute to understanding if clear and unambiguous policies have been established and these are communicated through relevant, purposeful documentation. Too much general information which has no clear relationship with the LEA's particular plans is as likely to inhibit the development of supportive attitudes as is too little specific information, and the impression that either the LEA has no clear strategy or, worse, that it has one but is not revealing it.

Training Methods

Trainers will need some expertise in organizing training activities for adults and the ability to select from a range of training methods and approaches relevant to different training objectives.

Timing

The amount and quality of time available for the first phase is critical. Whole days will produce a better return than the equivalent number of hours in 'twilight' sessions, and the time interval between this information transfer/awareness-raising stage and next phase – in school preparation – must not be over-long.

Above all, the LEA training strategy must consider how the necessary training can be provided whilst creating the minimum disruption to schools. Schools have been plunged into a pattern of training activities to support recent national initiatives (for example TVEI – the Technical Vocational Education Initiative – and GCSE) which have caused considerable discontinuity in the classroom. Appraisal is likely to be developed alongside extensive training programmes supporting the introduction of the National Curriculum and the associated assessment procedures, and it will be important to ensure that the phasing of schools into the training programme takes account of these other demands, and does not place an unrealistic burden on any one school.

As the emphasis in training shifts into the school, it is likely that continued impetus for the initiative will increasingly rely on support from a nominated person within the school, who in turn must have been trained to undertake this facilitative role. The benefits of common experience during Stage 1 should be apparent as the school begins, as a community, to plan for the introduction of appraisal. Again a number of factors would seem particularly important:

School Climate

If teachers are to move from an understanding of appraisal to a commitment to doing it, then they will need to have belief in the school's capacity to introduce appraisal fairly and professionally – the views, opinions and behaviour of senior staff will be critical in developing the necessary levels of trust and confidence.

Whole-school Engagement

The training should deliberately adopt a whole-school and school-specific stance. It should provide opportunity for the implications of appraisal to be fully explored in an open and cross-hierarchical environment.

Common Approaches

It is important that the broad approach to such activities as classroom observation is agreed – a set of ground rules which ensure parity of treatment for all staff and establish parameters for subsequent activity needs to be evolved.

Clearly Defined Roles

Each member of staff should understand the role(s) he/she will be required to undertake within appraisal and the expectations that accompany these roles.

Planning at School Level

A clear timetable for appraisal activity is needed within the school. This will need to be a realistic reflection of available time and resources, and it is important that monitoring takes place at school level, as any slippage within the programme is likely to have an adverse effect on teacher attitudes.

The need to support these activities within the school argues the need for a person (or persons) in the LEA whose full-time job is to facilitate and co-ordinate the LEA's appraisal strategy. It seems likely therefore that the LEA will need to identify an appropriate co-ordinator for teacher appraisal. The role of such a co-ordinator is discussed in more detail in Chapter 8 but it should be noted that though the co-ordinator may or may not undertake a direct training role, it is unlikely that the co-ordination role can be undertaken by a training team without the guidance of an appraisal co-ordinator.

If Stage 3 of the training process is to be realized, then some partnership between the LEA co-ordinator and an in-school co-ordinator will be necessary, since providing support from outside the school for this stage of the training process will be difficult. The sheer numbers involved (proportion of 'trainers' to teachers) imply that significant individualized support will not be available, though there will be a real need for 'coaching' (based on experience and feedback) during the early stages of the appraisal cycle. It is important that the requirements at this phase are clearly communicated to/discussed with school staff during Stage 2, so that some form of self-supporting scheme, which exploits the links between the training and practice, can be planned for. This scheme will need to be co-ordinated and monitored within the school. At this stage, the major learning will stem from involvement in live appraisal processes and will therefore be experiential. It would be unwise to assume that experience will automatically lead to competence. Harris has pointed out that experience is a 'good teacher' when:

new experiences are provided

intellectual activity is related to these new experiences

negative outcomes are minimised

timing of experiences promotes learning in useful sequence

confusion and frustration are prevented

feedback for correcting faulty performance is available

choices between alternative behaviour are made in systematic ways.

(Harris, 1980)

It is important, then, that the programme of support to individuals recognizes the need to view the appraisal process itself as a *training opportunity*, and allocates resources so that the criteria listed here can be met. In particular it should provide time for a school-based co-ordinator to discuss with teachers their experiences of appraisal, and to feed back into the planning process for the next cycle the lessons learned in this first run-through.

The balance of emphasis within responsibility for delivering the various stages of training is summarized in Figure 7.2.

This transfer of responsibility for training from an LEA co-ordinator via a group of trainers, into individual schools could be achieved through a 'cascade' strategy – and the relatively low cost of such a strategy may be a powerful factor in LEA deliberations. But if a cascade approach is to be used it will need to be done properly. The HMI evaluation of 'cascading' as a training strategy to support the introduction of GCSE (HMI, 1988) makes some useful points here. The cascade is most likely to prove effective where there is:

- firm central leadership and direction;

- clear LEA involvement in and support for the training activity;

- appropriate use made of 'experts' from external training providers;

- training extending to all staff, including headteachers;

- phased training allowing for reflection and review which can feed into the preparation of future training programmes.

As with other training strategies, the support available *after* the point when the process spreads into schools will be critical – attention will need to be given to how the development of good practice in school can be nurtured, learnt from, and disseminated to all staff involved.

Monitoring Training Activity

The appraisal training programme will need to be accompanied by monitoring activities in at least three dimensions. First, it will be important to ensure that the LEA's training strategy is actually being implemented. This will mean establishing a system which provides rapid and accurate feedback on whether the training activity is taking place as planned. In particular the monitoring system will need to be able to identify whether the following are as planned:

- the timing of individual training events;

- the phasing of training activities both across and within schools;

- the attendance/involvement of appropriate staff;

- the co-ordination of training activity with other support activities (such as the distribution of key documentation);

- the co-ordination of training activity for appraisal with other INSET demands and commitments.

Stage	Main Content Areas	Main Responsibility for Delivery
1	Information about appraisal	LEA co-ordinator + Central training team
	Information about LEA scheme	
	Information about knowledge and skills required to undertake the various activities	(+ 'Practitioners' from schools which are further along the road)
	Opportunity to begin skills development in simulated/role-play situations	
2	Analysis of where the school is in relation to appraisal	LEA co-ordinator + School co-ordinator
	Understanding school plan for introduction of appraisal including:	
	Roles: who will appraise whom? Tasks: what activities will this involve? Procedures: how will these activities be conducted? Timing: when will these occur? Documentation: what records will be kept? Use: what use will be made of data?	
3	Skills development	School co-ordinator + team of appraisers within the school
	Self-assessment Classroom observation Giving 'feedback' Appraisal dialogue Target setting Writing up	

Figure 7.2 *The delivery of appraisal training.*

Second, the training programme itself will need to be evaluated. This evaluation should encompass both the content and method of training activities, but who will be involved and how needs to be agreed locally. Nevertheless, in each case a number of issues will have to be considered and a list of the decisions about evaluation which will be required may be useful (see Figure 7.3).

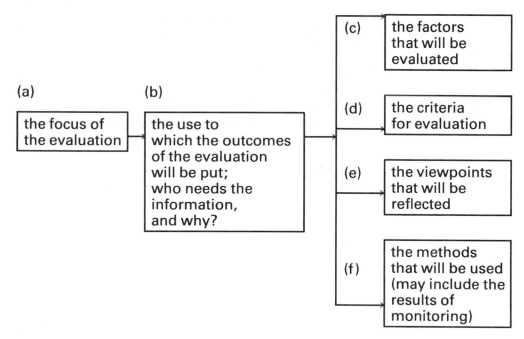

Figure 7.3   *Decisions which need to be made in evaluating training*
Source: Carroll and Nuttall (1989)

Third, there will need to be some monitoring of how the outcomes of teachers' appraisals influence the broader staff development strategies of school and LEA. Though this is a longer-term process it is nevertheless vital, and so attention should be given to this issue from the outset. In particular, there should be a commitment to follow up the impact of appraisal over a number of years and deliberately to seek out data about how the appraisal process relates generally to the long-term development of teachers and specifically to the effectiveness of other forms of training and development.

THE EXPERIENCE OF THE PILOT LEAs

Training in the appraisal pilot authorities has typically been well received, though both content and patterns have varied according to individual LEA schemes and priorities. A number of areas have emerged, nevertheless, where experience has been common across the LEAs.

First, the balance of training between appraisers and appraisees. Though the amount of training made available to the respective groups varied between pilot LEAs, appraisees consistently showed more positive attitudes towards appraisal and seemed better able to collaborate with appraisers to generate positive outcomes from appraisal processes when they received equal training. Further, they seemed readier to appreciate the 'learning' outcomes as ones they too had a stake in securing, rather than taking a passive view of the observation or interview session as something which was essentially done *to* them. Though there are clear resource implications for the start-up phase, taking appraisee training as seriously as appraiser training seems to bring dividends.

Second, and linked to this, is the need to offer training support for *all* aspects of the appraisal cycle. The pilot experience showed that assumptions about what teachers can do without, at least, orientation and more commonly specific training, are tenuous. Self-assessment, and knowing how to 'debrief' following classroom observation sessions are particular examples where the necessary skills had not been addressed, even though the activities had been 'covered' during training.

Third, a training method which offers opportunities for 'coaching' (practice-related feedback, discussion and further practice) seems most effective, though this was not always employed. This meant that teachers' real experiences within appraisal were crucial learning opportunities, and many teachers stressed the need for time and resources to be made available within the training strategy for this process to be carried through with colleagues. This would also validate the role of all members of staff as potential training resources for one another.

Fourth, training seems to increase in effectiveness where teachers are able to relate the 'messages' from appraisal training to school needs and LEA policies. So there needs to be a close fit between these, which is underlined by linking training to activities ongoing at classroom, school and LEA levels.

Finally, it is important to remember that other groups within the wider education community (for example advisers/inspectors, school governors) also need training about the LEA's appraisal scheme, and their own potential involvement in it.

SUMMARY OF KEY POINTS

The introduction of teacher appraisal will require the support of a training programme for *all teachers and headteachers* which both addresses the specific needs and processes of the LEA's particular scheme and relates to the wider LEA INSET strategy.

The planning and design of an appraisal training programme should

- reflect the descriptions of good INSET practice available in the literature;
- have a clear relationship to the LEA's overall staff development philosophy;
- be in harmony with and integrated into the LEA's staff development programme.

Training will need to address

- what teachers need to know about appraisal;
- what teachers need to feel about appraisal;
- what teachers need to be able to do within appraisal.

The effectiveness of training will be influenced by

- the perceived 'credibility' of those involved in training *as trainers and as practitioners*;
- the quality, amounts and relevance of information, training materials, and support documentation;

- the variety and appropriateness of training methods;
- the time available for and the timing of training activities.

Within the particular school training will need to

- be planned and sequenced to minimize disruption;
- provide opportunities for whole-school discussion of the requirements and implications of appraisal;
- generate consistent approaches and practices amongst appraisers;
- provide clear definitions of roles and expectations;
- recognize that the most important learning opportunities will arise from actual experience;
- support and consolidate good practice as it emerges

The training programme will need to be monitored

- at LEA level, to ensure that training plans and policies are being implemented;
- at participant level, so that the content and methods of training can be evaluated;
- at school and LEA levels, to ensure that the outcomes of appraisal have a long-term influence on staff development priorities and strategies.

Chapter 8

Managing Appraisal

The complexities of the issues discussed so far serve to underline that the management of teacher appraisal will be an important determinant of its success. This management function can be identified as necessary at two distinct levels, those of the LEA and of individual schools. At minimum this process must ensure adequate resourcing, co-ordination of individual effort and integration of appraisal processes, and produce outcomes contributing to the wider development strategy of the LEA.

CONTEXT

Bolam, pointing out that generalizations about how innovation in education can best be managed need to be viewed with extreme caution, nevertheless produces a useful summary of the major findings from published research:

> it should involve adaptive and continuing planning by the major participants and interest groups involved, giving an opportunity to adapt the goals and content of the innovation and providing mechanisms for feedback on progress;
>
> people in key leadership roles (for example, heads, advisers and chief education officers) should be overtly supportive and participate directly when appropriate;
>
> staff training should be provided in a relevant and continuing form, should give specific and practical 'how to do it' information, where possible provided by peers and practitioners and where appropriate in an on-the-job or classroom setting;
>
> continuing external support should be provided and should be both practical and personal;
>
> there should be opportunities for members of the target user group to develop and modify the innovation locally by adapting the materials and by learning about the innovation's characteristics and developing a sense of 'owning' it;
>
> 'a critical mass' of people involved should be developed so that individuals do not feel isolated but can meet together with like-minded enthusiasts as a team for discussion, information sharing and training.
>
> (Bolam, 1984)

Joan Dean, in figures which probably already underestimate the current requirements, indicates the scale of schoolteacher appraisal and the accompanying resource management problems:

> The second Suffolk study suggests an overall cost of £125 per teacher and within the range £600–£1,100 per headteacher. This includes the cost of initial training which will become less after the first programme. The figures include observation of three 40-minute lessons, half an hour for writing up and the equivalent of an hour and three quarters interview with each teacher. Headship

appraisal includes the costs of three people spending between nine and 17 hours in observation, reading and interviewing for each school, plus clerical time.

On this basis, in an authority with 50 secondary schools and 400 primary schools staffed by 6,000 teachers, the cost of teacher and headteacher appraisal will thus be over £1 million.

(Dean, in Fidler and Cooper, 1988)

Clearly, in a climate where there is ever-increasing competition for limited resources, it is vital that the huge sums invested in teacher appraisal show some return. This will, in turn, require effective management by both LEAs and schools.

Before considering the specifics of management role and tasks at these levels, it is perhaps worthwhile to consider briefly what the term 'management' implies. Drucker (1955) is credited with the definition of the management role which has been most influential in determining both our understanding of the managerial process and the components of management training over the past 30 years. His analysis of what it means to manage suggested five linked, but nevertheless distinct, components:

Planning – the process of identifying goals and objectives and indicating how these can be achieved within available resources.

Organizing – the process of analysing the range of activities which need to go on and allocating these to groups and individuals.

Monitoring – the process of checking actual outcomes against plans and where necessary modifying plans in the light of experience.

Communicating and Motivating – providing the right kind of information and relevant incentives so that individuals want to fulfil their part in the plan.

Developing Staff – ensuring that there are opportunities for people to develop and if possible finding ways which enable them to develop themselves via their daily work experience.

Though this list is rather different from the typical job description for LEA co-ordination roles, it provides a useful focus for thinking about the management of the teacher appraisal initiative.

Planning at both LEA and school levels will be a vital determinant of success, and in particular is more likely to be effective if those managing appraisal start with a clear vision of what appraisal should look like when fully implemented, and working back from there, make decisions about the necessary activities, resources and strategies for realizing this plan. The alternative 'incremental' approach which favours individual steps, one at a time, towards a poorly articulated goal has not proved conspicuously successful over the years.

Organizing, too, requires a clear understanding of both the structures and the staffing required if objectives are to be realized; above all this requires a mutual acceptance of the empowerment of individuals as a crucial aspect of effective human enterprise.

Monitoring is most effective when this empowerment is in place, so that each individual is in a position to monitor his or her own progress towards the objective and to adjust accordingly, rather than remaining reliant on the intervention (and the patronage) of a co-ordinator who, having put so much effort into 'writing the book' now wants to 'make the film' (the management of TVEI pilot projects amply demonstrates the limitations of this strategy).

Motivating is perhaps the most neglected of managerial functions. In education this is often explained away as a consequence of working with 'professionals' who, in theory at least, are self-motivating. Unfortunately there is little research evidence that teachers as a group are less in need of support for and recognition of their efforts than any other. There is also a history of schools being described as 'opting into' initiatives when we should perhaps more accurately say that the headteacher, not the staff, has volunteered. Thus a school's involvement in a development project does not necessarily imply a commitment from teachers.

It will be most important in the development of meaningful appraisal schemes that the individual teachers *want* to engage in the appraisal processes because of the real benefits they can see in this for themselves and for their pupils. A major function for those managing appraisal locally will be to build this desire.

Development will also be a high priority for management of an appraisal scheme. This development, as Drucker indicated, will need to extend beyond visible training activities. It is desirable that a management strategy be evolved to support teacher appraisal which fully acknowledges the importance of teacher self-development once the scheme is under way, and which continues to use supportive management strategies both from outside and inside the school to stimulate this process.

MANAGEMENT AT LEA LEVEL

The functions referred to above will probably need to be shared (though not equally) within the LEA amongst three parties: a designated senior officer of the LEA, a co-ordinator for teacher appraisal, and some form of steering group or working party. A possible division of tasks to be managed between these parties is set out here.

Designated Senior Officer

The designated senior officer will need to be a major point of contact between teacher appraisal implementation projects and the policy-making machinery of the LEA. A major responsibility will be to ensure that an appraisal scheme has been developed which is consistent both with any possible national requirements and with the particular context, policies and opportunities within the LEA. A vital aspect of this role will be to ensure that the objectives of the LEA scheme once established are properly resourced and therefore realistic in terms of time scales and costs. In fulfilling this requirement the objectives and operating parameters for the LEA co-ordinator will be identified. A second aspect of the designated officer's responsibilities will be to manage the co-ordinator's efforts within this framework. It is most likely that the officer fulfilling this role will also bear major responsibility for ensuring that appraisal is integrated into the LEA's wider policy and planning rhythms. This will mean ensuring that the demands of appraisal (particularly the training) are balanced alongside those of other national/LEA initiatives and that the data emerging from the appraisal process at school level is used to inform the LEA's future management strategy, particularly with regard to in-service training and development.

A further dimension might involve direct involvement in the selection/nomination of appraisers for headteachers, though the detailed planning for headteacher appraisal is probably best carried out by the co-ordinator.

It is clear that any coherent LEA scheme must include some provision for a complaints procedure. Each LEA therefore will need to establish appropriate machinery and though much of this can be expected to operate at school level it will be wise to lodge ultimate responsibility for overseeing complaints procedure with this officer.

The LEA Co-ordinator(s)

The appraisal scheme will need to be managed on a day-to-day basis and it is unlikely that in all but the smallest LEAs any senior officer would be able to find time to take on this additional area of responsibility. It seems likely that the LEAs will wish to appoint an appraisal co-ordinator (or possibly, in larger authorities, co-ordinators amongst whom the various tasks would be shared). Five main tasks seem appropriate at this level within the management structure. First, the major liaison role with schools. This should include written as well as oral communication, and so the co-ordinator should bear the major responsibility for the preparation and distribution of any documentation (whether general or specific) which the LEA wishes to make available to schools. Second, the co-ordinator will need to develop a detailed plan for the timing of appraisal implementation and the phasing-in of schools, though this of course must be feasible within the parameters referred to earlier. Third, co-ordinators will need to organize (and possibly contribute to) the delivery of training to support teacher appraisal: the training and deployment of trainers drawn from the LEA's teaching force. Fourth, the co-ordinator will need to organize headteacher appraisal. Finally, the co-ordinator will be well placed to provide advice on the progress and outcome of appraisal as it develops and so can provide an important informational input to whatever monitoring or planning machinery the LEA has established.

Steering/Working Party

As the successful implementation of appraisal is both a sensitive and an important issue to all partners in the education community, it is desirable that some form of steering group or working party should be established. The membership of this steering group should represent the spread of interested parties, including teacher associations. Its role would be seen as advisory rather than executive, though potentially such a group would have much to offer to the planning process and it may well be that this is also the most appropriate 'home' for the commissioning and interpretation of local evaluation activity.

MANAGEMENT AT SCHOOL LEVEL

Appraisal brings with it a need for management at the school level, within the context set by the LEA's policies. Though LEA co-ordinators will have an important role to play in supporting appraisal activity in schools, it is not possible to 'manage' implementation from outside the school. The weight of managing the introduction of appraisal will therefore fall on headteachers in the first instance, though in all but the smallest schools it seems likely that this role will be delegated to an appropriate member of the school's senior management team. This in-school management function will embrace a number of tasks.

Planning for Appraisal

It will be necessary to plan the introduction of appraisal extremely carefully. School-based activity will need to be sequenced alongside the training programme offered to staff; the various stages of the appraisal process will need to be sensibly phased throughout the year; those activities requiring cover/causing disruption to the timetable will need particular attention. Obviously the specific difficulties vary with school size, though the sorts of difficulty encountered may be more similar across schools than is often realized. Thus in the smallest schools for example, where the headteacher is likely to be the only appraiser but carries a full teaching commitment, and in large secondary schools, where an individual head of department has to fit in the appraisal of perhaps half a dozen members of staff, the disruption to the appraiser's own teaching programmes is a common problem.

Organizing Appraisal

Individual members of staff will need to be very clear about what appraisal will involve. It is vital that each person is fully aware of the demands appraisal will make upon them, as both appraisers and appraisees, and that they are thoroughly informed, prepared and supported to respond to these demands. In particular the planning and organizing which they, in turn, will have to carry out needs to be underlined. Wherever possible, it would seem desirable to consult with staff about how appraisal can best be organized within the particular school. Thus, once the overall plan showing the major requirements, resource provision and constraints is mapped out, it should be published to encourage active participation in decisions about organization. This is a major communication role of the school-level co-ordinator.

Monitoring Appraisal

It will be necessary to ensure that plans and timetables, once agreed, are met. This implies systematic logging of the various stages in the appraisal process, and periodic review. Again, although specific problems may seem related to school size – and it is obviously a more complex managerial operation in the larger school – the types of deviation that occur are remarkably similar, and it would be unwise to assume that in a smaller school there is no need to formalize these processes. Indeed, it may well be that the need for systematic planning and monitoring is greatest in the school where the headteacher is also a full-time class teacher and the sole appraiser in the school, as these circumstances often conspire to produce neglect.

It will also be important, where appraisers other than the headteacher are involved, to monitor the process of pairing appraisers and appraisees, and to ensure that a legitimate process of appeal is available to staff who are unhappy about either the choice of appraiser or the outcome of appraisal.

Developing Positive Attitudes

Though the potential benefits of appraisal are considerable, these will not necessarily be apparent to teachers, many of whom are already working under intense pressure, and whose time and attention are being competed for by several other major initiatives and reforms. It is important that teachers are able to understand where appraisal fits into their working lives, both logistically and philosophically, and that they are able to see it as a process that will help them to tackle the very wide range of demands currently being made on them, and as a vehicle to help them develop their professional skills in responding to these demands. If this is to be achieved then appraisal will need to be introduced sensitively and handled professionally, and the school co-ordinator will have a major responsibility to ensure that this happens. Key factors here will be the ability to demonstrate appropriate commitment from senior staff, to respond to and alleviate anxieties amongst teachers, to ensure that data produced from appraisal processes is used to influence school-level decision making and to initiate/support appropriate follow-up activity in individual cases.

Supporting Staff Development

As noted in Chapter 7, the most important areas of training for appraisal will be encountered when teachers start to participate in it. Though formal, off-the-job training to support the introduction of appraisal should identify those areas (for example the appraisal interview) where interpersonal competence will be most vital, and it is possible to incorporate some 'simulation' activities into initial training to give staff a feel for the sorts of situation they may find themselves in and the skills which will be most helpful, the major learning experiences will be actual appraisal interviews in which staff are involved. The school co-ordinator therefore will need to remind (and perhaps reassure) staff that all participants in the appraisal process are engaged in a significant learning experience. Effort should be made in each school to reflect upon that experience, to distil from it those lessons which seem most important and to spread emerging patterns of knowledge and skill which most often seem associated with good practice to all members of staff. It is particularly important that this process be managed in the early cycles, though there is likely to be a continuing need to promote discussion about this issue even amongst an 'experienced' staff who have worked through the appraisal cycle a number of times.

A second area of concern is staff development arising from the *outcomes* of appraisal, rather than the process itself. As mentioned previously, it is important for both the credibility of the appraisal system and to ensure that maximum benefit is derived from it that subsequent decisions about INSET priorities are informed by data made available via the appraisal process. Where the headteacher is the only appraiser, gathering together this data will not pose problems, though demonstrating that it is being acted upon remains important. In the large school, some mechanism will be required for analysing the data to identify common needs and concerns, whilst continuing to guarantee confidentiality. The school co-ordinator will need to consider how such needs and concerns can be conveyed from appraisers into the school INSET planning machinery. Though there is unlikely to be one best model here, it would seem important that whatever model is used has the support and confidence of teachers, and so co-ordinators may need to consult widely with staff in developing appropriate systems for processing and transferring data.

Liaising with the LEA

The school-level co-ordinator will be the principal point of contact on appraisal between school and LEA. So it is likely that this person will work closely with the LEA co-ordinator(s) and plan jointly with him/her for the introduction of appraisal into the school. Effective communication between the LEA and school is vital, as it is clearly desirable that there is always someone within the school who can interpret and explain the LEA's scheme and its training strategy. It is also desirable that LEA co-ordinators have access to feedback from schools, so that they are constantly able to evaluate their strategies and modify these as appropriate in the light of real experience. School co-ordinators are the natural source of this feedback.

ISSUES FOR LEAs AND SCHOOLS

There are a number of issues for those managing teacher appraisal which, although they have consequences for decision making at each level referred to, need to be resolved in a wider LEA context.

Resourcing Strategy

The resource implications of teacher appraisal are considerable. Whilst this undoubtedly entails several 'new' activities for LEAs and schools, it also covers a number of aspects that are currently going on within the education system, so the introduction of appraisal is unlikely to be fully funded. How resources are currently being used, for example, to identify INSET priorities or to fund classroom observation as a developmental activity may be difficult to establish, and more difficult to redirect. There is a need, in the short term, to evolve a clear resource strategy which delineates the time and resources directed into appraisal activities at LEA, school and teacher levels. Clear direction on this will need to be built into any LEA scheme, and both the amount and pattern of resourcing indicated must be realistically met through LEA provision. Though the designated LEA officer will have a central role in negotiating the resource requirement and monitoring its use and adequacy, both LEA and school co-ordinators will need a clear resource budget and clear basis for decision making within that budget. There will inevitably be a need to adjust patterns of resourcing within existing LEA budget headings to accommodate appraisal, and this needs to be initiated and monitored at the highest level within the LEA.

The Role of Officers and Governors

The part to be played by officers (including advisers and inspectors) in the appraisal process needs to be clarified from the outset. It is anticipated that the main involvement, initially, will be in headteacher appraisal and it is necessary both to define the nature of this involvement and to provide training for it. In the longer term, advisers may well have a role in supporting/providing follow-up to teacher appraisal – this too needs careful thinking through so that there is a consistent LEA policy and a consistent approach from officers in the individual case.

There has also been a fundamental change in the educational landscape since the ACAS agreement was drawn up. A major new feature of this landscape will be the replacement of the LEA by the governing body as the teachers' employer. Already many governing bodies are showing great interest in headteacher appraisal, and some in teacher appraisal. As yet examples of real involvement in the process tend to be both extremely local and by consent. It is necessary to consider how governor involvement is likely to increase in coming years, and to incorporate this involvement into the LEA strategy if at all possible to ensure that individual schools feel that they are being treated equally and fairly.

The Use Made of Appraisal Data

This has two aspects. First, the access to records themselves. Who will have access, and in what circumstances, is likely to be covered in local guidelines. But there will still be a managerial responsibility for storing and keeping secure any records of appraisal, and monitoring them in accordance with employee legislation and/or local guidelines. Though apparently a simple management task, this is one which is profoundly important to teachers, and a clear policy, matched by the physical resources needed to store and secure records in accordance with the policy, will be an important determinant of teachers' confidence.

Second, there is the question of how existing INSET planning processes can be made responsive to the accumulating data on needs and priorities which will be emerging at school and LEA level. Some clear, early decision about the relationship between teacher appraisal and teacher INSET planning needs to be seen as integral to a whole-LEA development strategy.

THE EXPERIENCE OF THE SCHOOL TEACHER APPRAISAL PILOT SCHEME

A number of common threads have emerged from the experiences of the six pilot authorities relating to management at both LEA and school levels.

LEA Level

Relationships   A common issue in the pilot schemes has been the need to define the relationships between those involved in the appraisal process. This has been particularly apparent in headteacher appraisal, where confusion over roles is more likely to be problematic both because of the lack of a clear line management structure above headteachers and the involvement of two or three persons as appraisers, and because of the need to collect data from other informed sources. Headteachers involved as appraisers of colleagues have been particularly keen to see the relationships and responsibilities of those involved defined, to ensure that the process remains thoroughly professional in approach.

Phase-related Knowledge and Experience   The pilot schemes have demonstrated the benefits of a co-ordination team which has within it direct experience of the phases of education represented within the LEA's school population. Though it remains desirable in terms of managerial accountability to have a single named co-ordinator, assistant or associated co-ordinators bringing with them different, relevant expertise into a co-ordination team offer significant benefits, not least where co-ordinators have a direct role in headteacher appraisal. It seems likely then that all but the smallest of LEAs will find it worthwhile to seek such an arrangement.

Link between Appraisal and Management Development   It is in the nature of categorically funded development work that a separate 'industry' is established within the LEA. Appraisal has therefore been treated as a 'single issue' development because of dedicated funding, rather than because it makes most sense to introduce it in that way. Indeed in the pilot LEAs there was increasing recognition that appraisal needed to be integrated into the LEA's broader management development strategy, not least because much of the training could serve general as well as specific needs. In some of the pilot authorities, appraisal has, in the post-pilot phase, been 'repatriated' into the LEA's management training structure; in others the appraisal co-ordinators have found their roles widened to tackle management development in the new context set by teacher appraisal. In either case the message is clear – LEAs need to think carefully about the full range of management development offered and see appraisal training as one part of this process.

Need for Continuing Support   Though appraisal training should be integrated into the LEA's overall provision, nevertheless there remains a need for an LEA co-ordinator to provide ongoing support and maintenance of appraisal activity in schools. The need to ensure integration should not be used as a reason for failing to make specific provision to support appraisal, but as a reason for ensuring that the appraisal co-ordinator is part of a team planning for LEA management development and not an isolated function.

School Level

Resources   Though resources in the pilot schemes have proved adequate, schools have typically been more generously treated than could be sustained on a national basis. Experience from across the pilot LEAs suggests that there are very real worries about the time required to do appraisal well, and how this time will be found on an ongoing basis in schools. This is clearly a major issue for school co-ordinators.

Disruption   Though teachers who have experienced appraisal in the pilot schemes are overwhelmingly positive about the process, a constant source of anxiety has been the disruption to the appraiser's teaching programme it has occasioned. Though some of this is inevitable, there is a strong feeling amongst pilot LEAs that where the burden can be lessened, it should be.

(Thus for example, there would be very strong support for the designation of a national training day for some of the initial training, as this would alleviate at least some of the disruption.) School co-ordinators will need to ensure that the school's implementation scheme is phased in in the way that does least damage to the curriculum experiences of pupils.

Monitoring   There has been a limited number of examples of large secondary schools within the pilot schemes, but the evidence available suggests that in the larger school planning for appraisal needs to be carried out alongside timetabling for the coming year if it is to minimize disruption. This brings with it a significant monitoring problem, as it is then necessary to have some way of 'triggering' activities at the appropriate point in the cycle and of ensuring that some individuals and departments are not falling behind due to other pressures. Working out a sensitive but effective system of monitoring progress will therefore be a vital function of the school co-ordinator.

Link with INSET Planning   If appraisal is to be effective it must be seen to influence INSET planning, and the school must therefore be able to respond, as resources become available, to agreed, identified needs. There is a strong case for linking the appraisal co-ordinator's role with the INSET co-ordinator's role, as has been done successfully in a number of pilot schools. However, it is important to recognize that the management role of the co-ordinators, as outlined in Chapter 8, is considerable, and so it should not be assumed that the co-ordination of appraisal can be accreted to the functions of the existing staff development co-ordinator (where one exists) – positive selection of individuals competent to meet the challenges of the role will be vital if the process is to be successful.

SUMMARY OF KEY POINTS

If appraisal is to contribute to the development of teachers and schools it will need to be carefully managed to ensure that it provides 'value for money' whilst minimizing the demands on teachers and the disruption of pupil learning experiences.

The management of teacher appraisal will need to be co-ordinated

- at LEA level;

- at school level.

The management process will need to ensure that at both levels teacher appraisal is

- planned – with identified goals and objectives and realistic resourcing;

- organized – so that individuals and groups are clear about their roles and the expectation placed upon them;

- monitored, so that plans and organizations can be adapted and modified in light of accumulating experience;

- able to offer appropriate stimulus/incentives for teachers to want to become meaningfully involved;

- developmental – creating opportunities for teachers to build and grow through direct experience.

The management strategy should clarify

- the roles of officers and governors in the appraisal process;

- the uses which will be made of data emerging from the appraisal process;

- the policy on access to appraisal data.

Chapter 9

Appraisal, Professional Development and School Improvement

In this final chapter we wish to stand back a little from the particulars of appraisal and to look at it in a more general way, from a developmental perspective. The implicit theme of the book has been 'appraisal for professional development' and that is certainly the approach to appraisal we wish to encourage. We also feel that appraisal has wider implications for development and it is to these themes that we now turn.

Appraisal does not exist in isolation and its long-term impact on teacher performance seems likely to depend on how far it is integrated with other forms of review and development. Teacher appraisal, headteacher appraisal, whole-school review, school development plans, curriculum planning and INSET planning are all related and if linked in a coherent and co-ordinated strategy would transform the school's capacity for change. But to reach the point where these activities are integrated will for some schools involve considerable changes in ethos or culture.

In this chapter we look at a number of aspects of this integration and change. In the following section we review some of the background to teacher, school and LEA development. We then discuss some of our findings on school development from the School Teacher Appraisal Pilot Study. In conclusion we examine the school improvement potential of teacher appraisal.

APPRAISAL AND DEVELOPMENT

It is perhaps predictable, but all the same regrettable, that we are least informed about the development phase of appraisal. In one sense development is implicit in all of the activities discussed in this book; so for example the teacher researcher and reflective practitioner approaches to self-evaluation have an obvious action/improvement orientation. So too do most forms of classroom observation. In this section we want to draw together and review briefly some ways in which appraisal can be explicitly linked to development at the level of the teacher, the school and the LEA.

Teacher Development

The most effective way of linking teacher development to appraisal is through the use of data-gathering methods that have a developmental focus. We have already mentioned the importance of this in relation to Stenhouse and Schon's notions of the 'teacher researcher' and 'reflective practitioner' respectively. There are other forms of collaborative appraisal that encourage teachers to establish, and work together in, a supportive and critical community, many of which we have already described.

Despite the rhetoric of collaboration, one of our major concerns is that those responsible for planning appraisal and for encouraging development often act on the basis of an overly rational conception of human behaviour. They seem to forget, or not to realize, that any change or development at an individual level involves learning, and that learning is often difficult and uncomfortable. Fullan (1985) has suggested a series of implications for the individual who is involved in innovation and change:

1   that change takes place over time;

2   that the initial stages of any significant change always involve anxiety and uncertainty;

3   that ongoing technical and psychological support assistance is crucial if the anxiety is to be coped with;

4   that change involves learning new skills through practice and feedback – it is incremental and developmental;

5   that the most fundamental breakthrough occurs when people can cognitively understand the underlying conception and rationale with respect of 'why this new way works better';

6   that organisational conditions within the school (peer norms, administrative leadership), and in relation to the school (e.g. external administrative support and technical help) make it more or less likely that the process will succeed;

7   successful change involves pressure, but it is pressure through interaction with peers and other technical and administrative leaders.

Appraisal, as we have noted, is currently an innovation and will remain so for some time. Our argument is that if effective change and development are to occur as a consequence of appraisal these implications for individual change need to be understood and incorporated into the planning processes.

School Development

Models for such school development are still not widespread, although we do know that it occurs as the result of collaborative action within a mutually agreed framework of action. The best-known British example of such a framework of action is that provided by the GRIDS project mentioned in Chapter 2 (McMahon et al., 1984; Abbott et al., 1988). The point of referring to GRIDS again is twofold. First, the GRIDS approach to school-level evaluation provides a framework for individual staff appraisal. As was seen in the Cumbria LEA appraisal pilot, the two can fruitfully go hand in hand. Second, GRIDS also provides a framework for school improvement (Bollington and Hopkins, 1989). There are now a number of other similar approaches, such as DION/SIGMA, IMTEC/FOCUS and the IDP process in common use in many of British schools (Hopkins, 1988).

These school review processes have much in common with the more general research-based approaches to school improvement that have recently been developed. The models of school improvement developed by Joyce et al. (1983), Loucks-Horsley and Hegert (1985), Bollen and Hopkins (1987), and Leithwood et al. (1987) all follow a similar pattern. They are useful in showing how strategies for school improvement such as appraisal and school review might be applied in a developmental way.

The current interest in school development planning provides a strategy for linking appraisal, school review and a variety of national and local initiatives together in a relatively coherent and practical way. The history of school self-evaluation suggests that the method is most successful when:

- it has a development orientation;

- it is linked to practical and useful changes at the school/classroom level; and

- teachers are skilled in its use.

School development plans require similar pre-conditions and provide a means of taking a more holistic view of school development. A simple diagram showing the positive relationship of school development plans, school self-evaluation and appraisal is seen in Figure 9.1.

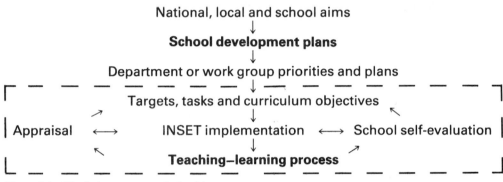

Figure 9.1   *The infrastructure of school improvement*

The activities within the dotted rectangle coexist and interact to provide an infrastructure for school improvement (Hopkins, forthcoming). In practice, of course, they do not occur sequentially and are not as discrete as the figure suggests. The recent DES-sponsored booklet on *Planning for School Development* (Hargreaves *et al.*, 1989) gives detailed advice to schools on ways in which development plans can be constructed and used to link together a variety of change initiatives at the school level.

LEA Development

LEA development is at the same time both crucial and elusive. The LEA needs to provide the shelter conditions for school and individual teacher development. In particular it needs to provide resources, direction, support and, particularly in the current climate, protection from innovation overload. There is unfortunately little research on the role of the LEA in change, although the work of Fullan (1982, 1985) and Purkey and Smith (1985) provide useful exceptions. A number of general guidelines can be drawn from this literature. If an LEA is successfully to introduce an appraisal scheme then it should:

- take the school as the focus of change and the school culture as the ultimate target of policy;

- encourage the school head and staff to engage in a process of review prior to embarking on appraisal;

- provide resources, especially time and training, to support and nurture the process;

- maximize local responsibility for the innovation whilst recognizing the responsibility of higher levels;

- provide leadership in the form of policy direction, and also plan for extension.

This is of course easier said than done; as Wise *et al.* (1985, p. 70) comment:

> The implementation of any school policy, including a teacher evaluation policy, represents a continuous interplay among diverse policy goals, established rules, and procedures, intergroup bargaining and value choices, and the local institutional context. The political climate of the school system, the relationship of the teachers; organisation of district management, the nature of other educational policies and operating programmes in the district, and the size and structure of the system and its bureaucracy all influence appraisal procedures.

This quotation has a particular relevance for the British situation at the present time. As LEAs are working towards defining and implementing policies for appraisal, so they are finding individuals and schools experimenting with the process and adapting the policy in use. The development of a coherent national and LEA policy on school development plans may well provide a key to harnessing this energy into a more unified direction.

TEACHER APPRAISAL, SCHOOL IMPROVEMENT AND THE CHANGE PROCESS

In her optimistic paper on the school improvement potential of American teacher evaluation schemes, Milbrey McLaughlin (1986) covers similar territory to ours. She claims that despite the accountability and evaluative overtones of American appraisal schemes, they also contain the potential for school improvement. Given the commitment to professional development through appraisal as exemplified in the NSG report (1989), the potential for genuine school improvement in the UK should be even greater.

McLaughlin cites the experience of a number of school districts which have adopted teacher evaluation practices based on improved observational and diagnostic skills in those involved in the appraisal process. In these districts observers are trained to observe classroom practices, assess teacher solutions to classroom problems, gauge the quality of teacher–student interactions and analyse the structure of the teaching–learning process. Observers trained in this way, she claims, acknowledge 'the conditional nature of teacher effectiveness and focus on individual teacher judgments and choices within broad and widely held categories for effective teaching' (1986, p. 164). Such a skill-based process supports school improvement because it affects factors that are fundamental to how teachers and heads go about their jobs and how well they carry out their responsibilities for teaching and management.

McLaughlin (1986, p. 170) continues to outline the conditions 'essential to a teacher-evaluation program that can contribute substantially to school improvement'. Her list is similar to ours:

- extensive and regular training;

- resources for appraisers;

- teacher participation in the design of appraisal programmes;

- explicit LEA support and involvement;

- integrating with other organization and curriculum initiatives.

It is heartening to find another major national evaluation coming to similar conclusions to the one we were involved with. But as always the implementation of these ideas is not easy. Implementation, even of good-quality and commonsense ideas does not proceed on auto-pilot.

As part of the work during the teacher appraisal pilot we looked at the strategies used in various LEAs to facilitate the implementation of what for many teachers represented an innovation, with consequent and considerable changes in their ways of working. The strategies we saw included a concern with climate setting, awareness raising, committed leadership, training and support. Taken together those strategies can ensure the successful introduction of appraisal. Another approach that has facilitated the implementation of appraisal is whole-school review. As we have discussed this particular aspect of the evaluation work earlier in the book and in detail elsewhere (Bollington and Hopkins, 1989), there is no need to rehearse the arguments again – except perhaps in one respect: that successful implementation requires a working knowledge of the innovation and change process.

We have already argued that to many appraisal is a major innovation. As Bolam (1975) and Fullan (1982) have quite correctly pointed out, the success of an innovation depends on the achievement and balancing of a number of factors. Most lists of the factors associated with successful innovation include the following:

- *the characteristics of the innovation*, e.g. the need for the change, its clarity, scope and complexity, and the quality of materials;

- *the characteristics at the LEA level*, e.g. establishing policy, providing resources and creating appropriate shelter conditions;

- *the characteristics at the school level*, e.g. the culture of the school, its capacity to plan and act, and community support;

- *the characteristics and activities of key actors*, e.g. teachers, heads and LEA officials;

- *the characteristics of the external environment*, e.g. the availability of additional funding, the role of teacher associations, and the quality of external consultancy;

- *the characteristics of the strategies for innovation*, e.g. the quality of training, a system for monitoring and feedback, and an understanding of the process of change.

We have already discussed most of these factors except perhaps for the process of change itself.

The innovation process is generally considered to consist of three overlapping phases: initiation, implementation and institutionalization (Miles, 1986). These predictable passages have different characteristics and require different strategies for success to be achieved. For example, during the initiation phase, to be successful the innovation, in our case appraisal, needs to be clearly articulated, have an active advocate, a forceful mandate, and be comple-mented by extensive training. During the implementation phase appraisal needs to be well co-ordinated, have adequate and sustained external support, have ownership increasingly spread throughout the school, and provide rewards for those involved (for example early success, supply cover, positive feedback). During the institutionalization phase, appraisal will need to be embedded in the school organization, tied into classroom practice, have widespread use in school and LEA, and be supported by a cadre of local trainers. If appraisal is viewed as an innovation in this sense then school development is likely to occur at the teacher, school and LEA levels.

CODA

We conclude by arguing for a stronger linkage between school development plans, whole-school review, appraisal and in-service training. There are signs that these somewhat disparate activities are beginning to come together. The NSG report (1989) in encouraging schools to develop approaches appropriate to their own organization, and to the individuals within it, is pointing the way forward. Such suggestions are particularly useful when they are coupled with advice on school development planning. Schools need the freedom to plan and act, within the context of course, of LEA support and monitoring. But it is, in the end, only at the level of the school that planning, curriculum development, school review, teacher appraisal, classroom observation and in-service training can be integrated and co-ordinated in such a way as to foster the development of the school as a creative 'thinking' and dynamic institution. Many of the schools we have worked with on the appraisal pilot, for example, have experience of these alternative methods. The dramatic changes in the governance of British schools in recent years provide both the need and the opportunity for many more schools to adopt strategies like these in their efforts to enhance the quality of their pupils' education.

Appendix 1:

Summary of the National Steering Group Report

School Teacher Appraisal: A National Framework
Report of the National Steering Group on the School Teacher Appraisal Pilot Study (HMSO, 1989). Our Summary of the Report's Recommendations

The report builds on the earlier ACAS report and the pilot study experience and makes the following suggestions:

1 LEAs should have the statutory *responsibility for securing the appraisal of teachers* in LEA-maintained schools.

2 LEAs should also be responsible for the *training* needed to support the implementation of appraisal.

3 LEAs should be required to implement appraisal for all those employees and school staff who are on teachers' conditions of service, with the exception of probationary, licensed and articled teachers (although it is recognized that the scheme used will need to be modified for advisory/peripatetic teachers).

4 *The appraiser of a teacher should be designated by the headteacher* (unless the headteacher is the appraiser) and should, wherever possible, be a person who already has management responsibility for the teacher.

5 *Headteachers should be appraised by two appraisers*, appointed in the case of LEA-maintained schools by the chief education officer (CEO). (In the case of voluntary aided or special agreement schools, the CEO should appoint appraisers in consultation with the governing body and take into account the view of the professional Diocesan advisers, where applicable.) One of the appraisers should have 'experience as a head relevant to current conditions' in the phase in which the appraisee works and if one of the appraisers is required to take the lead in appraisal then this head or ex-head should have that role. (Serving heads should be involved as appraisers of no more than three heads at any one time.) One of the appraisers should be a 'professional officer of the LEA'.

6 Heads and teachers should be appraised through a *two-year cycle* of activities (see Figure A1.1).

7 The *LEA will need to be in a position to respond to and to support the outcomes of appraisal* in line with the ACAS principles (ii)–(vi).

8 *LEAs should consider and prepare guidance on criteria* to be used in appraisal, *in consultation with teachers*.

9 *Access to agreed appraisal statements* should be restricted to the appraisee, the appraiser(s), the headteacher of the school, the CEO and LEA officers or advisers specifically designated by the CEO for this purpose. In the case of appraisal statements of headteachers, one copy of the statement should always be sent to the CEO.

10 LEAs should, after appropriate consultation, establish the 'shelf-life' of appraisal statements.

11 LEAs should establish a *complaints machinery* available to heads/teachers if they consider that either the manner in which their appraisal was conducted or the conclusions reached were 'unreasonable'.

12 LEAs should indicate their commitment to appraisal, consult widely on the development of the LEA scheme, provide teachers/heads with appropriate explanatory materials, raise awareness about appraisal and implement it in conjunction with the National Curriculum and school development plans.

13 LEA officers and advisers should be given appropriate training for their roles in the appraisal process, including monitoring its operation and participating in headteacher appraisal. Governors should receive information about appraisal in their training. Trainers from within the LEA should receive training for this role.

14 The NSG argues for an *extra closure day* during the implementation period for appraisal training. The NSG argues for appraisal to be implemented over the period 1990–4.

15 LEAs should arrange for *the monitoring and evaluation* of their appraisal scheme.

16 Teacher appraisal is initially expected to take 16 hours of the appraiser's time and 12 hours of the appraisee's over two years, reducing subsequently to 11.5 hours and 8.25 hours. The figures for headteacher appraisal are: appraiser 1–23 hours (17.5); appraiser 2–10 hours (7); appraisee 16.5 hours (12). The NSG estimate that 4.5 hours of cover will be needed by each teacher being appraised plus 5.95 hours for each teacher appraiser. The costs of headteacher appraisal relate to how far appraisers are seconded; if appraisers are not seconded, cover might be needed for 8.6 hours for each appraiser. (These cover figures relate to the 'ongoing' phase.)

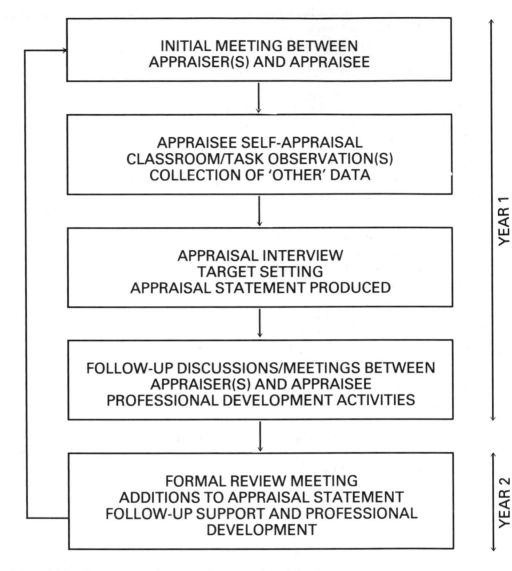

Figure A1.1   *Components in the appraisal process: a biennial cycle*
Source: NSG (1989), p. 9, reproduced with the permission of the Controller of Her Majesty's Stationery Office

Appendix 2:

Guidance and Code of Practice on the Collection of Information for Teacher and Headteacher Appraisal*

1 This guidance and Code of Practice covers the collection of information for teacher and headteacher appraisal other than through classroom observation.

GENERAL PRINCIPLES

2 Information collection for the purpose of the appraisal of a teacher or headteacher should be designed to assist discussion in an appraisal interview having the purposes set out [earlier in the NSG Report].

3 Where it has been agreed that the appraisal should concentrate on specific aspects of the appraisee's job, information collection should likewise concentrate on those aspects.

4 Appraisers should act with sensitivity to all concerned and should not exhibit any bias in collecting information.

5 Those giving information should not be put under any pressure save that of relevance and accuracy.

6 General comments should be supported by specific examples.

7 Interviews for the purpose of information collection should be held on a one-to-one basis.

8 Any information received anonymously should not be used.

9 Information which does not relate to the professional performance of a teacher or head-teacher should not be sought or accepted.

10 Appraisees should not adopt an obstructive attitude to reasonable proposals for the collection of appropriate information.

11 Neither appraisers nor appraisees should act in any way that is likely to threaten the trust and confidence on both sides upon which successful appraisal depends.

BACKGROUND INFORMATION

Teacher Appraisal

12 The teacher's appraiser must be familiar with relevant national and LEA policies and requirements.

* From NSG (1989), reproduced with the permission of the Controller of Her Majesty's Stationery Office.

13 The appraiser will also need to acquire a range of background information appropriate to the appraisee's wider professional responsibilities, e.g. the school's statements of aims and objectives, pastoral arrangements, equal opportunities policies, or departmental policies.

14 The appraiser should obtain copies of the teacher's job description and the previous appraisal statement.

Headteacher Appraisal

15 The headteacher's appraisers must be familiar with current national and LEA policies and requirements with regard to curriculum, special needs, equal opportunities, staffing and cover, disciplinary and grievance procedures and other such matters relating to school management.

16 They will also need a wide range of background information about the school and its context including:

> curricular policies;
>
> general organization and deployment of staff;
>
> composition and organization of the governing body;
>
> links with home, outside bodies and other schools;
>
> the pattern of meetings with staff and with parents;
>
> school activities and routines including assessment and recording systems, examination results, calendar of events;
>
> staff appraisal and development arrangements and arrangements for induction and probation;
>
> financial and management systems.

This information will need to be assembled by appraisee heads, who may provide any supplementary information they wish.

17 The appraisers should obtain copies of the headteacher's job description and of the previous appraisal statement.

Other Guidance to the Appraiser

18 The appraiser should agree with the appraisee at the initial meeting what information it would be appropriate to collect for the purpose of the appraisal, from what sources and by what methods.

19 When interviewing people providing information as part of an appraisal, the appraiser should explain the purpose of the interview and the way in which information will be treated.

20 Those giving information should be encouraged to make fair and considered comments which they are prepared to acknowledge and to substantiate if required.

21 Any written submissions should remain confidential to the author, the appraiser and the appraisee.

22 Those offering significantly critical comments should be asked to discuss them directly with the appraisee before they are used as appraisal information. (The substance of grievance or disciplinary proceedings should never be used in the appraisal process.)

23 Except where personal opinion is specifically sought (for example where an appraiser is attempting to gauge staff reactions to a particular innovation), care should be taken to ensure that information is sought and presented in an objective way.

Recommended Reading

Our own reading about appraisal led to a review of research based on the experience of appraisal in a variety of settings, for example commercial, industrial and educational (Hopkins and Bollington, 1989). This early work convinced us of the value of appraisal for professional development and the importance of clarifying the purposes and processes of appraisal. In this review we paid particular attention to North American experience, because of the longstanding American experience of appraisal.

The picture which emerged from this reading was a story of what not to do. A number of North American writers, in particular Arthur Wise and Milbrey McLaughlin (Wise and Darling-Hammond, 1984; Wise *et al*., 1985; McLaughlin, 1986, 1988) and the contributors to the edition of *Educational Leadership* (44 (7)) devoted to teacher appraisal, drew attention to the failure of many appraisal schemes to lead to school or individual development. These writers present a critique of schemes designed to provide checklists to assess minimum competence. They argue that such accountability models of appraisal quickly degenerate into bureaucratic rituals. By contrast they argue for the development of schemes concerned with school improvement and individual growth.

The English and Welsh experience has developed rather differently. From the days of *Those Having Torches* (Suffolk Education Dept, 1985) and of the ACAS *Report* (1986) to the present, the trend in the 'accountability–development' debate has been in favour of appraisal for development. Certainly appraisal for professional development and individual growth featured in the School Teacher Appraisal Pilot Study of 1987–9. The National Steering Group's Report, *School Teacher Appraisal – a National Framework* (NSG, 1989) presents a case for a national appraisal framework, based on the ACAS principles and concerned with the development of teachers and the effective management of schools. Appraisal is seen as a continuous, systematic and positive process. The report also draws attention to the cost implications of the proposed scheme, estimating the costs of operating appraisal in the ongoing phase at between £36.4 and £40.5 million. The pilot study generated a number of other seminal documents about appraisal. Among these are the Cambridge Institute of Education *Report on the Evaluation of the School Teacher Appraisal Pilot Study* (Bradley *et al*., 1989) and the documentation produced during the course of the STAPS by the pilot LEAs and the National Development Centre, for example the report from the York conference (McMahon, 1988). These reports, in reviewing the issues connected with appraisal, drew attention to the wide range of benefits it can produce.

At the time of writing, we are entering a period of consultation about the nature of a national appraisal scheme. This follows the decision of the Secretary of State to delay the issue of regulations setting up a compulsory system. In addition to the NSG report, he has cited the HMI report on appraisal (HMI, 1989) as a key document in the consultation period. This raises a number of issues about appraisal. Notable among these are the practical difficulties of operating appraisal in areas where there is a shortage of teachers and high staff turnover; the suitability of the proposed timescale for the introduction of appraisal; the lack of clarity concerning the links between appraisal and pay and appraisal and the identification of performance difficulties.

As the momentum towards the spread of appraisal has increased, a number of practical guides have appeared. Some deal with the process generally (e.g. Wragg, 1987), whereas others relate to particular stages in the process (e.g. Hewton, 1988). Alongside these practical guides, a number of books have appeared, which are based on research into appraisal. Notable here is the work of Turner and Clift (1988).

The journeys of both our own reading and the development of appraisal in the UK are not yet complete. Nevertheless, we feel that the wide experience on which we have drawn in this book should be useful background to those in schools and LEAs designing, for the present voluntarily, their own professional development or appraisal schemes.

References

Abbott, R. *et al.* (1988) *GRIDS Handbooks* (5 vols), 2nd edition. York: Longman.

ACAS (1986) *Report of the Appraisal/Training Working Group*. London: ACAS.

Acheson, K. and Gall, M. (1980) *Techniques in the Clinical Supervision of Teachers*. New York: Longman.

Adair, J. (1983) *Effective Leadership*. London: Pan.

Allinson, C. W. (1977) 'Training in performance appraisal interviewing', *The Journal of Management Studies*, **May**, 179–91.

Armstrong, M. (1977) *A Handbook of Personnel Management Practice*. London: Kogan Page.

Association of Teacher Educators (1988) *Teacher Assessment*. Virginia, USA: Association of Teacher Educators.

Bolam, R. (1975) 'The management of educational change. Towards a conceptual framework', in Houghton, V., McHugh, R. and Morgan, C. (eds) *Management in Education*. London: Ward Lock Educational.

Bolam, R. (1984) 'Some practical generalisations about the change process', in Campbell, G. (ed.) *Health Education and Youth: A Review of Research and Development*. Lewes: Falmer Press.

Bollen, R. and Hopkins, D. (1987) *School Based Review: Towards a Praxis*. Leuven, Belgium: ACCO.

Bollington, R. and Hopkins, D. (1987) *Teacher Appraisal for Professional Development: A Review of Research*. Cambridge: CIE.

Bollington, R. and Hopkins, D. (1989) 'School-based review as a strategy for the implementation of teacher appraisal and school improvement', *Educational Change and Development*, **10**(1), 8–17.

Bradley, H. W. *et al.* (1988) *Analysis of the Questionnaire Survey of Teacher Attitudes to Appraisal*. Cambridge: CIE.

Bradley, H. W. *et al.* (1989) *Report on the Evaluation of the School Teacher Appraisal Pilot Study*. Cambridge: CIE.

Brophy, J. E. and Good, T. L. (1986) 'Teacher behaviour and student achievement', in Wittrock, M. C. (ed.) *Handbook of Research on Teaching*, 3rd edition. New York: Macmillan.

Bunnell, S. (ed.) (1987) *Teacher Appraisal in Practice*. London: Heinemann.

Buttram, J. L. and Wilson, B. L. (1987) 'Promising trends in teacher evaluation', *Educational Leadership*, **44**(7), 4–6.

Carroll, S. and Nuttall, S. (1989) *The Staff Development Manual Volume 3*. Lancaster: Framework Press.

Cogan, M. (1973) *Clinical Supervision*. Boston: Houghton Mifflin.

Conley, D. T. (1987) 'Critical attributes of effective evaluation systems', *Educational Leadership*, **44**(7), 60–4.

Cooper, C. L. and Makin, P. (1984) *Psychology for Managers*, 2nd edition. London: British Psychological Society/Macmillan.

References

Coopers and Lybrand (1988) *Local Management of Schools*. London: Coopers and Lybrand.

Croll, P. (1986) *Systematic Classroom Observation*. Lewes: Falmer Press.

Cumbria LEA (1988) *Guide to the Cumbria Teacher Appraisal Project Pilot Study*. Whitehaven: Cumbria County Council.

Darling-Hammond, L., Wise, A. E. and Pease, S. R. (1983) 'Teacher evaluation in the organisational context: a review of the literature', *Review of Educational Research*, **53**(3), 285–328.

Day, C. (1987) 'The relevance of classroom research about the observation of teachers in classrooms for appraisal purposes'. Paper presented to BERA Conference, Nottingham: University of Nottingham.

Day, C. W. and Moore, R. (ed.) (1986) *Staff Development in the Secondary School: Management Perspectives*. London: Croom Helm.

DES (1983) *Teaching Quality*. London: HMSO.

DES (1985) *Better Schools*. London: HMSO.

Doyle, W. (1987) 'Research on teaching effects as a resource for improving instruction', in Wideen, M. and Andrews, I. (eds) *Staff Development for School Improvement*. Lewes: Falmer Press.

Drucker, P. F. (1955) *The Practice of Management*. London: Heinemann.

Fenstermacher, G. D. (1978) A philosophical consideration of recent research on teacher effectiveness. In Shulman, L. S. (ed.) *Review of Research in Education*, vol. 6. Itasca, Ill.: F. E. Peacock.

Fidler, B. and Cooper, R. (eds) (1988) *Staff Appraisal in Schools and Colleges*. Harlow: Longman.

Fullan, M. (1982) *The Meaning of Educational Change*. Ontario: Oise.

Fullan, M. (1985) 'Change processes and strategies at the local level', *Elementary School Journal*, **85**(3), 391–421.

Fuller, B. *et al.* (1982) 'The organizational context of individual efficacy', *Review of Educational Research*, **52**(1), 7–30.

Galton, M. (1978) *British Mirrors*. Leicester: University of Leicester School of Education.

Gane, V. (1986) *Secondary Headteacher Appraisal: The Nub of Credibility*. Bristol: National Development Centre for School Management Training (NDC–SMT).

Gibbons, M. and Phillips, G (1980) *Self Education*. Vancouver: Challenge Education Associates.

Gibbons, M. *et al.* (1980) *The Negotiated Learning Contract*. Vancouver: Challenge Education Associates.

Gill, D. (1977) *Appraising Performance*. London: Institute of Personnel Management.

Goldhammer, R. *et al.* (1980). *Clinical Supervision: Special Methods for the Supervision of Teachers*, 2nd edition. New York: Holt, Rinehart and Winston.

Greenwich, Connecticut, Committee on Effective Teaching (1983) *Report from Committee on Effective Teaching*.

Guskey, T. (1986) 'Staff development and the process of teacher change', *Educational Researcher*, **15**(5), 5–12.

Hammersley, M. (ed.) (1986) *Controversies in Classroom Research*. Milton Keynes: Open University Press.

Hargreaves, D. H. *et al.* (1989) *Planning for School Development*. London: HMSO.

Harris, B. (1980) *Improving Staff Performance through In-service Education*. Boston: Allyn and Bacon.

Hewton, G. (1988) *The Appraisal Interview*. Milton Keynes: Open University Press.

HMI (1982) *The New Teacher in School*. London: HMSO.

HMI (1988) *Report by HM Inspectors on a Critique of the Implementation of the Cascade Model Used to Provide INSET for Teachers in Preparation for the Introduction of the GCSE*. London: DES.

HMI (1989) *Development in the Appraisal of Teachers*. London: DES.

Hook, C. (1981) *Studying Classrooms*. Victoria: Deakin University Press.

Hopkins, D. (1985) *A Teacher's Guide to Classroom Research*. Milton Keynes: Open University Press.

Hopkins, D. (1986) *In-Service Training and Educational Development*. London: Croom Helm.

Hopkins, D. (1987) *Improving the Quality of Schooling*. Lewes: Falmer Press.

Hopkins, D. (1988) *Doing School Based Review*. Leuven, Belgium: ACCO.

Hopkins, D. (forthcoming) *School Improvement in an Era of Change*. London: Cassell.

Hopkins, D. and Bollington, R. (1989) 'Teacher Appraisal for Professional Development: a review of research', *Cambridge Journal of Education*, **19**(2), 163–82.

Hopkins, D. and Leask, M. (1989) 'Performance indicators and school development', *School Organisation*, **9**(1), 3–20.

Hopkins, D. and Norman, P. (1982) *Professional Development*. Vancouver: Challenge Education Associates.

Hosford, P. L. (ed.) (1984) *Using What We Know about Teaching*. Alexandria, Va.: Association for Supervision and Curriculum.

Hunter, M. (1980) 'Six types of supervisory conferences', *Educational Leadership*, **37**(5), 412.

James, E. J. F. (1972) *Teacher Education and Training (The James Report)*. London: HMSO.

Jones, A. (1987) *Leadership for Tomorrow's Schools*. Oxford: Blackwell.

Joyce, B. (ed.) (1990) *Changing School Culture through Staff Development*. Alexandria, Va.: ASCD.

Joyce, B. and Showers, B. (1980) 'Improving in-service training: the messages of research', *Educational Leadership*, **37**(5), 379–85.

Joyce, B. and Showers, B. (1988) *Student Achievement through Staff Development*. New York: Longman.

Joyce, B. and Weil, M. (1986) *Models of Teaching*, 2nd edition. Englewood Cliffs, NJ: Prentice-Hall.

Joyce, B. *et al.* (1983) *The Structure of School Improvement*. New York: Longman.

Kelly, M. (1988) *Occupational Stress amongst Headteachers and Principals*. Haywards Heath: National Association of Headteachers.

Knowles, M. (1975) *Self-Directed Learning*. Chicago: Association Press.

Knowles, M. S. (1986) *Using Learning Contracts*. San Francisco: Jossey-Bass.

Kyriacou, C. (1986) *Effective Teaching in Schools*. Oxford: Blackwell.

Kyriacou, C. and Newson, G. (1982) 'Teacher effectiveness: A consideration of research problems', *Educational Review*, **34**(1), 3–12.

LEAP I (Local Education Authorities Project, Module I) (1989) *School Change and Challenge*. London: BBC.

Leithwood, K. *et al.* (1987) *The School Improvement Process*. Toronto: Ontario Ministry of Education.

Likert, R. (1967) *The Human Organization*. New York: McGraw-Hill.

Locke, E. A. (1978) 'The ubiquity of the technique of goal-setting in theories and approaches to employee motivations', in Steers, R. M. and Porter, L. W., *Motivation and Work Behavior*. New York: McGraw-Hill.

Loucks-Horsley, S. and Hegert, L. (1985) *An Action Guide to School Improvement*. Andover, Mass. and Oxford, Ohio: National Staff Development Council.

Loucks-Horsley, S. *et al.* (1987) *Continuing to Learn*. Andover, Mass: The Network.

Main, A. (1985) *Educational Staff Development*. London: Croom Helm.

McLaughlin, M. W. (1986) 'Teacher evaluation and school improvement', in Leiberman, A. (ed.) *Rethinking School Improvement: Research, Craft and Concept*. New York: Teachers College Press.

McLaughlin, M. W. and Pfeifer, R. S. (1988) *Teacher Evaluation: Improvement Accountability and Effective Learning*. New York: Teachers College Press.

McMahon, A. (1988) Consortium of School Teacher Appraisal Pilot Scheme – Progress on Appraisal: Interim Report. NDC: Bristol.

McMahon, A. *et al.* (1984) *Guidelines for Review and Internal Development in Schools*. York: Longman.

Meyer, H. H. *et al.* (1965) 'Split roles in performance appraisal', *Harvard Business Review*, **43**(1), 123–9.

Miles, M. (1986) *Research Findings on the Stages of School Improvement*. Center for Policy Review, New York: mimeo.

Millman, J. (ed.) (1981) *Handbook on Teacher Evaluation*. Beverly Hills, Calif.: Sage.

Montgomery, D. (1984) *Evaluation and the Enhancement of Teaching Performance*. Kingston Polytechnic: Learning Difficulties Project.

Morgan, C. and Turner, G. (1976) *E321: Management in Education: Unit 14* (Role, the Educational Manager and the Individual in the Organisation). Milton Keynes: Open University.

Natriello, G. and Dornbusch, S. M. (1980–1) 'Pitfalls in the evaluation of teachers by principals', *Administrator's Notebook*, **29**(6).

Newcastle LEA (1987) *STAFF handbooks*. Newcastle upon Tyne: Newcastle LEA.

NSG (National Steering Group for Teacher Appraisal) (1989) *School Teacher Appraisal – A National Framework*. London: HMSO.

Nuttall, D. (1986) 'What can we learn from research on teaching and appraisal?', in Dockerell, B. *et al.*, *Appraising Appraisal*. Birmingham: British Educational Research Association.

Office of Teacher Education and Certification and In-Service Staff Development (1983) *Domains of the Florida Performance Measurement System*. Tallahassee, Fla.: Office of Teacher Education, Certification and In-Service Staff Development.

Patterson, T. T. (1978) *Job Evaluation: A Manual for the Patterson Method*, vol. 2. London: Business Books.

Purkey, S. and Smith, M. (1985) 'School reform: the district policy implications of the effective schools literature', *Elementary School Journal*, **5**(3), 352–87.

Rudduck, J. (1981) *Making the Most of the Short Inservice Course*. London: Methuen Educational.

Salford LEA (1988a) *Appraisal: Consultative Document*. Salford: LEA.

Salford LEA (1988b) *Teaching Analysis and Support. Ten Steps*. Salford: LEA.

Salford LEA (1989) *Headteacher Appraisal Information*. Salford: LEA.

Schmuck, R. A. and Runkel, P. J. (1985) *The Handbook of Organisation Development in Schools*. Palo Alto, Calif.: Mayfield.

Schon, D. (1983) *The Reflective Practitioner*. New York: Basic Books.

Simon, A. and Boyer, E. (1975) *Mirrors for Behaviour: An Anthology of Classroom Observation Instrument*. Philadelphia: Research for Better School Inc.

Somerset LEA (1988a) *Pilot Light*. Bridgwater: Somerset County Council.

Somerset LEA (1988b) *Head Light*. Bridgwater: Somerset County Council.

Steadman, S. *et al.* (1989) *Setting Standards in Schools*. York: Longman for the School Curriculum Development Committee.

Steers, R. M. and Porter, L. W. (1983) *Motivation and Work Behaviour*, 3rd edition. New York: McGraw-Hill.

Stenhouse, L. (1975) *An Introduction to Curriculum Research and Development*. London: Heinemann.

Stenning, W. I. and R. (1984) 'The assessment of teachers' performance: some practical considerations', *School Organisation and Management Abstracts*, **3**, 77–9.

Stufflebeam, D. L. (1988) *The Personnel Evaluation Standards*. Beverly Hills, Calif.: Sage.

Suffolk Education Department (1985) *Those Having Torches*. Ipswich: Suffolk Education Department.

Suffolk Education Department (1987) *In the Light of Torches*. London: The Industrial Society.

Suffolk LEA (1988a) *Teacher Appraisal: A Practical Guide*. Ipswich: Suffolk County Council.

Suffolk LEA (1988b) *Notes of Guidance for Headteacher Appraisal*. Ipswich: Suffolk County Council.

Trethowan, D. (1987) *Appraisal and Target Setting: Handbook for Teacher Development*. London: Harper and Row.

Turner, G. and Clift, P. (1985) *A First Review and Register of School and College-based Teacher Appraisal Schemes*. Milton Keynes: Open University Press.

Turner, G. and Clift, P. (1988) *Studies in Teacher Appraisal*. Lewes: Falmer Press.

Wise, A. E. and Darling-Hammond, L. (1984) 'Teacher evaluation and teacher professionalism', *Educational Leadership*, **42**(4), 28–33.

Wise, A. E. *et al.* (1985) 'Teacher evaluation: a study of effective practices', *Elementary School Journal*, **86**(1), 61–121.

Wragg, E. C. (1987) *Teacher Appraisal: A Practical Guide*. London: Macmillan.

Name Index

'Fig' after a location reference denotes a figure in the text.

Subject Index

'Fig' after a location reference denotes a figure in the text.